50 Poland Ice Cream Recipes for Home

By: Kelly Johnson

Table of Contents

- Vanilla Ice Cream
- Chocolate Ice Cream
- Strawberry Ice Cream
- Raspberry Ice Cream
- Blueberry Ice Cream
- Cherry Ice Cream
- Coffee Ice Cream
- Hazelnut Ice Cream
- Almond Ice Cream
- Pistachio Ice Cream
- Mint Chocolate Chip Ice Cream
- Lemon Ice Cream
- Orange Ice Cream
- Mango Ice Cream
- Pineapple Ice Cream
- Coconut Ice Cream
- Black Forest Ice Cream (with cherries and chocolate)
- Tiramisu Ice Cream
- Caramel Ice Cream
- Salted Caramel Ice Cream
- Cookies and Cream Ice Cream
- Peanut Butter Ice Cream
- Nutella Ice Cream
- Stracciatella Ice Cream
- White Chocolate Raspberry Ice Cream
- Matcha Green Tea Ice Cream
- Elderflower Ice Cream
- Rose Ice Cream
- Lavender Honey Ice Cream
- Apple Pie Ice Cream
- Cheesecake Ice Cream
- Red Velvet Ice Cream
- Banana Nut Ice Cream
- Pina Colada Ice Cream
- S'mores Ice Cream

- Blueberry Cheesecake Ice Cream
- Gingerbread Ice Cream
- Cherry Cheesecake Ice Cream
- Cookies and Maple Syrup Ice Cream
- Carrot Cake Ice Cream
- Fig and Honey Ice Cream
- Pumpkin Pie Ice Cream
- Rice Pudding Ice Cream
- Rum Raisin Ice Cream
- Bourbon Pecan Ice Cream
- Cardamom Pistachio Ice Cream
- Earl Grey Tea Ice Cream
- Chai Spice Ice Cream
- Chocolate Chip Cookie Dough Ice Cream
- Neapolitan Ice Cream

Vanilla Ice Cream

Ingredients:

- 2 cups heavy cream
- 1 cup whole milk
- 3/4 cup granulated sugar
- Pinch of salt
- 1 vanilla bean (or 1 tablespoon vanilla extract)
- 6 large egg yolks

Instructions:

1. **Prepare the Base:**
    - In a medium saucepan, combine the heavy cream, whole milk, sugar, and salt. If using a vanilla bean, split it lengthwise with a knife and scrape out the seeds. Add both the seeds and the pod to the saucepan. Heat over medium heat, stirring occasionally, until the mixture is steaming and just begins to bubble around the edges (do not boil). Remove from heat.
2. **Temper the Eggs:**
    - In a separate bowl, whisk the egg yolks until smooth. Gradually whisk in about 1 cup of the hot cream mixture, a little at a time, to temper the eggs and prevent them from curdling.
3. **Combine and Cook:**
    - Pour the tempered egg mixture back into the saucepan with the remaining cream mixture. Cook over medium heat, stirring constantly with a heatproof spatula or wooden spoon, until the custard thickens slightly and coats the back of the spatula (about 5-7 minutes). Do not let it boil.
4. **Strain and Chill:**
    - Remove the vanilla bean pod (if used). Pour the custard through a fine-mesh sieve into a clean bowl to remove any bits of cooked egg or vanilla pod. Place the bowl in an ice bath or refrigerator until chilled completely, stirring occasionally.
5. **Churn:**
    - Once chilled, pour the custard into an ice cream maker and churn according to the manufacturer's instructions until the mixture reaches a soft-serve consistency.
6. **Freeze:**

- Transfer the churned ice cream to an airtight container, press a piece of parchment paper directly against the surface to prevent ice crystals from forming, and freeze until firm (at least 4 hours or overnight).
7. **Serve:**
    - Scoop and enjoy your homemade Vanilla Ice Cream!

This recipe yields creamy and delicious vanilla ice cream, perfect for enjoying on its own or alongside your favorite desserts.

Chocolate Ice Cream

Ingredients:

- 2 cups heavy cream
- 1 cup whole milk
- 3/4 cup granulated sugar
- Pinch of salt
- 6 ounces semi-sweet chocolate, chopped (or chocolate chips)
- 6 large egg yolks
- 1 teaspoon vanilla extract

Instructions:

1. **Prepare the Base:**
   - In a medium saucepan, combine the heavy cream, whole milk, sugar, and salt. Heat over medium heat, stirring occasionally, until the mixture is steaming and just begins to bubble around the edges (do not boil).
2. **Melt the Chocolate:**
   - Place the chopped chocolate in a heatproof bowl. Once the cream mixture is heated, pour it over the chocolate. Let it sit for a minute, then stir until the chocolate is completely melted and the mixture is smooth. Set aside.
3. **Temper the Eggs:**
   - In a separate bowl, whisk the egg yolks until smooth. Gradually whisk in about 1 cup of the warm chocolate mixture, a little at a time, to temper the eggs and prevent them from curdling.
4. **Combine and Cook:**
   - Pour the tempered egg mixture back into the saucepan with the remaining chocolate mixture. Cook over medium heat, stirring constantly with a heatproof spatula or wooden spoon, until the custard thickens slightly and coats the back of the spatula (about 5-7 minutes). Do not let it boil.
5. **Strain and Chill:**
   - Remove from heat and stir in the vanilla extract. Pour the custard through a fine-mesh sieve into a clean bowl to remove any bits of cooked egg. Place the bowl in an ice bath or refrigerator until chilled completely, stirring occasionally.
6. **Churn:**
   - Once chilled, pour the custard into an ice cream maker and churn according to the manufacturer's instructions until the mixture reaches a soft-serve consistency.

7. **Freeze:**
    - Transfer the churned chocolate ice cream to an airtight container, press a piece of parchment paper directly against the surface to prevent ice crystals from forming, and freeze until firm (at least 4 hours or overnight).
8. **Serve:**
    - Scoop and enjoy your homemade Chocolate Ice Cream! It's perfect for any occasion, and you can customize it by adding chocolate chips or chunks for extra texture if desired.

Strawberry Ice Cream

Ingredients:

- 1 pound fresh strawberries, hulled and sliced
- 3/4 cup granulated sugar, divided
- 1 tablespoon lemon juice
- 2 cups heavy cream
- 1 cup whole milk
- Pinch of salt
- 6 large egg yolks
- 1 teaspoon vanilla extract

Instructions:

1. **Prepare the Strawberries:**
   - In a bowl, combine the sliced strawberries, 1/4 cup of sugar, and lemon juice. Stir well and let sit at room temperature for about 30 minutes, stirring occasionally, until the strawberries release their juices.
2. **Blend the Strawberries:**
   - Transfer the strawberry mixture to a blender or food processor and blend until smooth. You can leave some chunks if you prefer more texture. Set aside.
3. **Prepare the Base:**
   - In a medium saucepan, combine the heavy cream, whole milk, remaining 1/2 cup of sugar, and salt. Heat over medium heat, stirring occasionally, until the mixture is steaming and just begins to bubble around the edges (do not boil).
4. **Temper the Eggs:**
   - In a separate bowl, whisk the egg yolks until smooth. Gradually whisk in about 1 cup of the warm cream mixture, a little at a time, to temper the eggs and prevent them from curdling.
5. **Combine and Cook:**
   - Pour the tempered egg mixture back into the saucepan with the remaining cream mixture. Cook over medium heat, stirring constantly with a heatproof spatula or wooden spoon, until the custard thickens slightly and coats the back of the spatula (about 5-7 minutes). Do not let it boil.
6. **Strain and Chill:**

- Remove from heat and stir in the vanilla extract. Pour the custard through a fine-mesh sieve into a clean bowl to remove any bits of cooked egg. Stir in the blended strawberry mixture.

7. **Chill Further:**
   - Place the bowl in an ice bath or refrigerator until chilled completely, stirring occasionally.
8. **Churn:**
   - Once chilled, pour the strawberry custard into an ice cream maker and churn according to the manufacturer's instructions until the mixture reaches a soft-serve consistency.
9. **Freeze:**
   - Transfer the churned strawberry ice cream to an airtight container, press a piece of parchment paper directly against the surface to prevent ice crystals from forming, and freeze until firm (at least 4 hours or overnight).
10. **Serve:**
    - Scoop and enjoy your refreshing and creamy Strawberry Ice Cream! It's perfect for summer and showcases the natural sweetness of fresh strawberries.

Raspberry Ice Cream

Ingredients:

- 12 ounces fresh raspberries
- 3/4 cup granulated sugar, divided
- 1 tablespoon lemon juice
- 2 cups heavy cream
- 1 cup whole milk
- Pinch of salt
- 6 large egg yolks
- 1 teaspoon vanilla extract

Instructions:

1. **Prepare the Raspberries:**
   - In a bowl, combine the raspberries, 1/4 cup of sugar, and lemon juice. Stir well and let sit at room temperature for about 30 minutes, stirring occasionally, until the raspberries release their juices.
2. **Blend the Raspberries:**
   - Transfer the raspberry mixture to a blender or food processor and blend until smooth. You can strain the mixture through a fine-mesh sieve to remove the seeds if desired. Set aside.
3. **Prepare the Base:**
   - In a medium saucepan, combine the heavy cream, whole milk, remaining 1/2 cup of sugar, and salt. Heat over medium heat, stirring occasionally, until the mixture is steaming and just begins to bubble around the edges (do not boil).
4. **Temper the Eggs:**
   - In a separate bowl, whisk the egg yolks until smooth. Gradually whisk in about 1 cup of the warm cream mixture, a little at a time, to temper the eggs and prevent them from curdling.
5. **Combine and Cook:**
   - Pour the tempered egg mixture back into the saucepan with the remaining cream mixture. Cook over medium heat, stirring constantly with a heatproof spatula or wooden spoon, until the custard thickens slightly and coats the back of the spatula (about 5-7 minutes). Do not let it boil.
6. **Strain and Chill:**

- Remove from heat and stir in the vanilla extract. Pour the custard through a fine-mesh sieve into a clean bowl to remove any bits of cooked egg. Stir in the blended raspberry mixture.

7. **Chill Further:**
    - Place the bowl in an ice bath or refrigerator until chilled completely, stirring occasionally.
8. **Churn:**
    - Once chilled, pour the raspberry custard into an ice cream maker and churn according to the manufacturer's instructions until the mixture reaches a soft-serve consistency.
9. **Freeze:**
    - Transfer the churned raspberry ice cream to an airtight container, press a piece of parchment paper directly against the surface to prevent ice crystals from forming, and freeze until firm (at least 4 hours or overnight).
10. **Serve:**
    - Scoop and enjoy your vibrant and creamy Raspberry Ice Cream! It's a perfect treat for any occasion, especially when fresh raspberries are in season.

Blueberry Ice Cream

Ingredients:

- 12 ounces fresh blueberries
- 3/4 cup granulated sugar, divided
- 1 tablespoon lemon juice
- 2 cups heavy cream
- 1 cup whole milk
- Pinch of salt
- 6 large egg yolks
- 1 teaspoon vanilla extract

Instructions:

1. **Prepare the Blueberries:**
    - In a saucepan, combine the blueberries, 1/4 cup of sugar, and lemon juice. Cook over medium heat, stirring occasionally, until the blueberries soften and release their juices, about 5-7 minutes. Remove from heat and let cool slightly.
2. **Blend the Blueberries:**
    - Transfer the cooked blueberry mixture to a blender or food processor and blend until smooth. You can strain the mixture through a fine-mesh sieve to remove any solids. Set aside.
3. **Prepare the Base:**
    - In a medium saucepan, combine the heavy cream, whole milk, remaining 1/2 cup of sugar, and salt. Heat over medium heat, stirring occasionally, until the mixture is steaming and just begins to bubble around the edges (do not boil).
4. **Temper the Eggs:**
    - In a separate bowl, whisk the egg yolks until smooth. Gradually whisk in about 1 cup of the warm cream mixture, a little at a time, to temper the eggs and prevent them from curdling.
5. **Combine and Cook:**
    - Pour the tempered egg mixture back into the saucepan with the remaining cream mixture. Cook over medium heat, stirring constantly with a heatproof spatula or wooden spoon, until the custard thickens slightly and coats the back of the spatula (about 5-7 minutes). Do not let it boil.
6. **Strain and Chill:**

    - Remove from heat and stir in the vanilla extract. Pour the custard through a fine-mesh sieve into a clean bowl to remove any bits of cooked egg. Stir in the blended blueberry mixture.
7. **Chill Further:**
    - Place the bowl in an ice bath or refrigerator until chilled completely, stirring occasionally.
8. **Churn:**
    - Once chilled, pour the blueberry custard into an ice cream maker and churn according to the manufacturer's instructions until the mixture reaches a soft-serve consistency.
9. **Freeze:**
    - Transfer the churned blueberry ice cream to an airtight container, press a piece of parchment paper directly against the surface to prevent ice crystals from forming, and freeze until firm (at least 4 hours or overnight).
10. **Serve:**
    - Scoop and enjoy your creamy and flavorful Blueberry Ice Cream! It's a wonderful way to enjoy the freshness of blueberries in a refreshing dessert.

Cherry Ice Cream

Ingredients:

- 2 cups fresh cherries, pitted and halved
- 3/4 cup granulated sugar, divided
- 1 tablespoon lemon juice
- 2 cups heavy cream
- 1 cup whole milk
- Pinch of salt
- 6 large egg yolks
- 1 teaspoon vanilla extract

Instructions:

1. **Prepare the Cherries:**
   - In a saucepan, combine the cherries, 1/4 cup of sugar, and lemon juice. Cook over medium heat, stirring occasionally, until the cherries soften and release their juices, about 5-7 minutes. Remove from heat and let cool slightly.
2. **Blend the Cherries:**
   - Transfer the cooked cherry mixture to a blender or food processor and blend until smooth. You can strain the mixture through a fine-mesh sieve to remove any solids. Set aside.
3. **Prepare the Base:**
   - In a medium saucepan, combine the heavy cream, whole milk, remaining 1/2 cup of sugar, and salt. Heat over medium heat, stirring occasionally, until the mixture is steaming and just begins to bubble around the edges (do not boil).
4. **Temper the Eggs:**
   - In a separate bowl, whisk the egg yolks until smooth. Gradually whisk in about 1 cup of the warm cream mixture, a little at a time, to temper the eggs and prevent them from curdling.
5. **Combine and Cook:**
   - Pour the tempered egg mixture back into the saucepan with the remaining cream mixture. Cook over medium heat, stirring constantly with a heatproof spatula or wooden spoon, until the custard thickens slightly and coats the back of the spatula (about 5-7 minutes). Do not let it boil.
6. **Strain and Chill:**

- Remove from heat and stir in the vanilla extract. Pour the custard through a fine-mesh sieve into a clean bowl to remove any bits of cooked egg. Stir in the blended cherry mixture.

7. **Chill Further:**
   - Place the bowl in an ice bath or refrigerator until chilled completely, stirring occasionally.
8. **Churn:**
   - Once chilled, pour the cherry custard into an ice cream maker and churn according to the manufacturer's instructions until the mixture reaches a soft-serve consistency.
9. **Freeze:**
   - Transfer the churned cherry ice cream to an airtight container, press a piece of parchment paper directly against the surface to prevent ice crystals from forming, and freeze until firm (at least 4 hours or overnight).
10. **Serve:**
    - Scoop and enjoy your creamy and flavorful Cherry Ice Cream! It's a delightful treat that captures the essence of fresh cherries in every bite.

Coffee Ice Cream

Ingredients:

- 2 cups heavy cream
- 1 cup whole milk
- 3/4 cup granulated sugar
- Pinch of salt
- 1/2 cup coarsely ground coffee beans (or instant coffee powder for a smoother texture)
- 6 large egg yolks
- 1 teaspoon vanilla extract

Instructions:

1. **Prepare the Coffee Infusion:**
    - In a medium saucepan, combine the heavy cream, whole milk, sugar, salt, and ground coffee beans (or instant coffee powder). Heat over medium heat, stirring occasionally, until the mixture is steaming and just begins to bubble around the edges (do not boil). Remove from heat and let steep for about 20-30 minutes to infuse the coffee flavor. Strain the mixture through a fine-mesh sieve into a clean bowl, pressing down on the coffee grounds to extract as much flavor as possible. Discard the coffee grounds.
2. **Prepare the Base:**
    - In the same saucepan (rinse if needed), reheat the coffee-infused cream mixture until steaming.
3. **Temper the Eggs:**
    - In a separate bowl, whisk the egg yolks until smooth. Gradually whisk in about 1 cup of the warm coffee-infused cream mixture, a little at a time, to temper the eggs and prevent them from curdling.
4. **Combine and Cook:**
    - Pour the tempered egg mixture back into the saucepan with the remaining coffee-infused cream mixture. Cook over medium heat, stirring constantly with a heatproof spatula or wooden spoon, until the custard thickens slightly and coats the back of the spatula (about 5-7 minutes). Do not let it boil.
5. **Strain and Chill:**
    - Remove from heat and stir in the vanilla extract. Pour the custard through a fine-mesh sieve into a clean bowl to remove any bits of cooked egg.
6. **Chill Further:**

- Place the bowl in an ice bath or refrigerator until chilled completely, stirring occasionally.
7. **Churn:**
    - Once chilled, pour the coffee custard into an ice cream maker and churn according to the manufacturer's instructions until the mixture reaches a soft-serve consistency.
8. **Freeze:**
    - Transfer the churned coffee ice cream to an airtight container, press a piece of parchment paper directly against the surface to prevent ice crystals from forming, and freeze until firm (at least 4 hours or overnight).
9. **Serve:**
    - Scoop and enjoy your creamy and aromatic Coffee Ice Cream! It's a wonderful treat with a rich coffee flavor that's perfect on its own or paired with desserts like brownies or chocolate cake.

Hazelnut Ice Cream

Ingredients:

- 2 cups heavy cream
- 1 cup whole milk
- 3/4 cup granulated sugar
- Pinch of salt
- 1/2 cup coarsely ground coffee beans (or instant coffee powder for a smoother texture)
- 6 large egg yolks
- 1 teaspoon vanilla extract

Instructions:

1. **Prepare the Coffee Infusion:**
     - In a medium saucepan, combine the heavy cream, whole milk, sugar, salt, and ground coffee beans (or instant coffee powder). Heat over medium heat, stirring occasionally, until the mixture is steaming and just begins to bubble around the edges (do not boil). Remove from heat and let steep for about 20-30 minutes to infuse the coffee flavor. Strain the mixture through a fine-mesh sieve into a clean bowl, pressing down on the coffee grounds to extract as much flavor as possible. Discard the coffee grounds.
2. **Prepare the Base:**
     - In the same saucepan (rinse if needed), reheat the coffee-infused cream mixture until steaming.
3. **Temper the Eggs:**
     - In a separate bowl, whisk the egg yolks until smooth. Gradually whisk in about 1 cup of the warm coffee-infused cream mixture, a little at a time, to temper the eggs and prevent them from curdling.
4. **Combine and Cook:**
     - Pour the tempered egg mixture back into the saucepan with the remaining coffee-infused cream mixture. Cook over medium heat, stirring constantly with a heatproof spatula or wooden spoon, until the custard thickens slightly and coats the back of the spatula (about 5-7 minutes). Do not let it boil.
5. **Strain and Chill:**
     - Remove from heat and stir in the vanilla extract. Pour the custard through a fine-mesh sieve into a clean bowl to remove any bits of cooked egg.
6. **Chill Further:**

- Place the bowl in an ice bath or refrigerator until chilled completely, stirring occasionally.
7. **Churn:**
    - Once chilled, pour the coffee custard into an ice cream maker and churn according to the manufacturer's instructions until the mixture reaches a soft-serve consistency.
8. **Freeze:**
    - Transfer the churned coffee ice cream to an airtight container, press a piece of parchment paper directly against the surface to prevent ice crystals from forming, and freeze until firm (at least 4 hours or overnight).
9. **Serve:**
    - Scoop and enjoy your creamy and aromatic Coffee Ice Cream! It's a wonderful treat with a rich coffee flavor that's perfect on its own or paired with desserts like brownies or chocolate cake.

Hazelnut Ice Cream

Ingredients:

- 1 cup whole milk
- 2 cups heavy cream
- 3/4 cup granulated sugar
- Pinch of salt
- 1 cup hazelnuts, toasted and finely ground
- 6 large egg yolks
- 1 teaspoon vanilla extract

Instructions:

1. **Prepare the Hazelnuts:**
    - Preheat your oven to 350°F (175°C). Spread the hazelnuts in a single layer on a baking sheet and toast them in the oven for about 10-12 minutes, or until fragrant and lightly browned. Remove from the oven and let cool. Once cool, rub the hazelnuts with a clean kitchen towel to remove as much of the skins as possible. Grind the hazelnuts finely in a food processor or blender. Set aside.
2. **Prepare the Base:**
    - In a medium saucepan, combine the whole milk, heavy cream, half of the sugar (about 6 tablespoons), and salt. Heat the mixture over medium heat, stirring occasionally, until it begins to steam and small bubbles form around the edges. Do not let it boil.
3. **Infuse the Hazelnuts:**
    - Stir the ground hazelnuts into the warm cream mixture. Let it steep off the heat for about 30 minutes to infuse the hazelnut flavor. After steeping, strain the mixture through a fine-mesh sieve or cheesecloth into a clean bowl, pressing down on the hazelnuts to extract as much flavor as possible. Discard the solids.
4. **Prepare the Custard:**
    - In a separate bowl, whisk together the egg yolks and the remaining sugar until well combined and slightly thickened.
5. **Temper and Cook the Custard:**
    - Gradually pour the warm hazelnut-infused cream mixture into the bowl with the egg yolks and sugar, whisking constantly, to temper the eggs. Pour the mixture back into the saucepan.
6. **Cook the Custard:**

- Cook the custard mixture over medium heat, stirring constantly with a wooden spoon or heatproof spatula, until it thickens slightly and coats the back of the spoon (about 5-7 minutes). Do not let it boil.

7. **Strain and Chill:**
    - Remove the custard from heat and stir in the vanilla extract. Strain the custard through a fine-mesh sieve into a clean bowl to remove any bits of cooked egg or hazelnut. Place the bowl in an ice bath or refrigerate until completely chilled, stirring occasionally.
8. **Churn:**
    - Once chilled, pour the hazelnut custard into an ice cream maker and churn according to the manufacturer's instructions until it reaches a soft-serve consistency.
9. **Freeze:**
    - Transfer the churned hazelnut ice cream into an airtight container, pressing a piece of parchment paper directly against the surface to prevent ice crystals from forming. Freeze for at least 4 hours or until firm.
10. **Serve:**
    - Scoop and enjoy your creamy and nutty Hazelnut Ice Cream! It's delicious on its own or paired with chocolate desserts for an extra indulgence.

Almond Ice Cream

Ingredients:

- 1 cup whole milk
- 2 cups heavy cream
- 3/4 cup granulated sugar
- Pinch of salt
- 1 cup almonds, blanched and finely chopped or ground
- 6 large egg yolks
- 1 teaspoon almond extract
- 1/2 cup toasted almond slices (optional, for garnish)

Instructions:

1. **Prepare the Almonds:**
    - If your almonds are not already blanched, blanch them by placing them in boiling water for about 1 minute, then immediately transferring them to ice water to cool. Remove the skins by gently squeezing each almond. Finely chop or grind the blanched almonds in a food processor or blender. Set aside.
2. **Prepare the Base:**
    - In a medium saucepan, combine the whole milk, heavy cream, half of the sugar (about 6 tablespoons), and salt. Heat over medium heat, stirring occasionally, until it begins to steam and small bubbles form around the edges. Do not let it boil.
3. **Infuse the Almonds:**
    - Stir the finely chopped or ground almonds into the warm cream mixture. Let it steep off the heat for about 30 minutes to infuse the almond flavor. After steeping, strain the mixture through a fine-mesh sieve or cheesecloth into a clean bowl, pressing down on the almonds to extract as much flavor as possible. Discard the solids.
4. **Prepare the Custard:**
    - In a separate bowl, whisk together the egg yolks and the remaining sugar until well combined and slightly thickened.
5. **Temper and Cook the Custard:**
    - Gradually pour the warm almond-infused cream mixture into the bowl with the egg yolks and sugar, whisking constantly, to temper the eggs. Pour the mixture back into the saucepan.
6. **Cook the Custard:**

- Cook the custard mixture over medium heat, stirring constantly with a wooden spoon or heatproof spatula, until it thickens slightly and coats the back of the spoon (about 5-7 minutes). Do not let it boil.

7. **Strain and Chill:**
   - Remove the custard from heat and stir in the almond extract. Strain the custard through a fine-mesh sieve into a clean bowl to remove any bits of cooked egg or almond. Place the bowl in an ice bath or refrigerate until completely chilled, stirring occasionally.

8. **Churn:**
   - Once chilled, pour the almond custard into an ice cream maker and churn according to the manufacturer's instructions until it reaches a soft-serve consistency.

9. **Freeze:**
   - Transfer the churned almond ice cream into an airtight container, pressing a piece of parchment paper directly against the surface to prevent ice crystals from forming. Sprinkle toasted almond slices on top if desired. Freeze for at least 4 hours or until firm.

10. **Serve:**
    - Scoop and enjoy your creamy and flavorful Almond Ice Cream! It's a wonderful treat with the nutty richness of almonds that pairs beautifully with desserts or is delightful on its own.

Pistachio Ice Cream

Ingredients:

- 1 cup shelled pistachios, unsalted
- 1 cup whole milk
- 2 cups heavy cream
- 3/4 cup granulated sugar
- Pinch of salt
- 6 large egg yolks
- 1 teaspoon vanilla extract
- Green food coloring (optional, for a more vibrant color)

Instructions:

1. **Prepare the Pistachios:**
    - In a food processor or blender, pulse the pistachios until finely chopped. You want them to be a coarse meal texture, not completely ground into powder. Set aside.
2. **Prepare the Base:**
    - In a medium saucepan, combine the whole milk, heavy cream, half of the sugar (about 6 tablespoons), and salt. Heat over medium heat, stirring occasionally, until it begins to steam and small bubbles form around the edges. Do not let it boil.
3. **Infuse the Pistachios:**
    - Stir the chopped pistachios into the warm cream mixture. Let it steep off the heat for about 30 minutes to infuse the pistachio flavor. After steeping, strain the mixture through a fine-mesh sieve or cheesecloth into a clean bowl, pressing down on the pistachios to extract as much flavor as possible. Discard the solids.
4. **Prepare the Custard:**
    - In a separate bowl, whisk together the egg yolks and the remaining sugar until well combined and slightly thickened.
5. **Temper and Cook the Custard:**
    - Gradually pour the warm pistachio-infused cream mixture into the bowl with the egg yolks and sugar, whisking constantly, to temper the eggs. Pour the mixture back into the saucepan.
6. **Cook the Custard:**

- Cook the custard mixture over medium heat, stirring constantly with a wooden spoon or heatproof spatula, until it thickens slightly and coats the back of the spoon (about 5-7 minutes). Do not let it boil.

7. **Strain and Chill:**
   - Remove the custard from heat and stir in the vanilla extract. Strain the custard through a fine-mesh sieve into a clean bowl to remove any bits of cooked egg or pistachio. Add a few drops of green food coloring if desired for a more vibrant color. Place the bowl in an ice bath or refrigerate until completely chilled, stirring occasionally.

8. **Churn:**
   - Once chilled, pour the pistachio custard into an ice cream maker and churn according to the manufacturer's instructions until it reaches a soft-serve consistency.

9. **Freeze:**
   - Transfer the churned pistachio ice cream into an airtight container, pressing a piece of parchment paper directly against the surface to prevent ice crystals from forming. Freeze for at least 4 hours or until firm.

10. **Serve:**
    - Scoop and enjoy your creamy and flavorful Pistachio Ice Cream! It's a delightful dessert that showcases the natural richness and nuttiness of pistachios.

Mint Chocolate Chip Ice Cream

Ingredients:

- 2 cups heavy cream
- 1 cup whole milk
- 3/4 cup granulated sugar
- Pinch of salt
- 2 cups fresh mint leaves, packed
- 6 large egg yolks
- 1 teaspoon vanilla extract
- 1 cup dark chocolate chips or chopped dark chocolate

Instructions:

1. **Infuse the Mint:**
   - In a medium saucepan, combine the heavy cream, whole milk, half of the sugar (about 6 tablespoons), and salt. Heat over medium heat, stirring occasionally, until it begins to steam and small bubbles form around the edges. Remove from heat, add the fresh mint leaves, and let steep for about 30 minutes to infuse the mint flavor. After steeping, strain the mixture through a fine-mesh sieve or cheesecloth into a clean bowl, pressing down on the mint leaves to extract as much flavor as possible. Discard the mint leaves.
2. **Prepare the Base:**
   - In the same saucepan (rinse if necessary), reheat the mint-infused cream mixture until steaming.
3. **Prepare the Custard:**
   - In a separate bowl, whisk together the egg yolks and the remaining sugar until well combined and slightly thickened.
4. **Temper and Cook the Custard:**
   - Gradually pour the warm mint-infused cream mixture into the bowl with the egg yolks and sugar, whisking constantly, to temper the eggs. Pour the mixture back into the saucepan.
5. **Cook the Custard:**
   - Cook the custard mixture over medium heat, stirring constantly with a wooden spoon or heatproof spatula, until it thickens slightly and coats the back of the spoon (about 5-7 minutes). Do not let it boil.
6. **Strain and Chill:**

- Remove the custard from heat and stir in the vanilla extract. Strain the custard through a fine-mesh sieve into a clean bowl to remove any bits of cooked egg. Place the bowl in an ice bath or refrigerate until completely chilled, stirring occasionally.

7. **Churn:**
   - Once chilled, pour the mint custard into an ice cream maker and churn according to the manufacturer's instructions until it reaches a soft-serve consistency.

8. **Add Chocolate Chips:**
   - During the last few minutes of churning, add the dark chocolate chips or chopped chocolate into the ice cream maker and continue to churn until evenly distributed.

9. **Freeze:**
   - Transfer the churned Mint Chocolate Chip Ice Cream into an airtight container, pressing a piece of parchment paper directly against the surface to prevent ice crystals from forming. Freeze for at least 4 hours or until firm.

10. **Serve:**
    - Scoop and enjoy your refreshing and creamy Mint Chocolate Chip Ice Cream! It's a classic flavor combination that's perfect for any occasion, especially on a hot day.

Lemon Ice Cream

Ingredients:

- 1 cup fresh lemon juice (about 4-5 lemons)
- Zest of 2 lemons
- 1 1/2 cups granulated sugar
- 2 cups heavy cream
- 1 cup whole milk
- Pinch of salt
- 6 large egg yolks
- 1 teaspoon vanilla extract

Instructions:

1. **Prepare the Lemon Base:**
    - In a medium saucepan, combine the lemon juice, lemon zest, and 1 cup of sugar. Heat over medium heat, stirring occasionally, until the sugar is dissolved and the mixture is steaming. Remove from heat and let it cool slightly.
2. **Prepare the Cream Mixture:**
    - In another medium saucepan, combine the heavy cream, whole milk, remaining 1/2 cup of sugar, and salt. Heat over medium heat, stirring occasionally, until it begins to steam and small bubbles form around the edges. Do not let it boil.
3. **Temper the Eggs:**
    - In a separate bowl, whisk together the egg yolks until smooth. Gradually whisk in about 1 cup of the warm cream mixture, a little at a time, to temper the eggs.
4. **Combine and Cook:**
    - Pour the tempered egg mixture back into the saucepan with the remaining cream mixture. Cook over medium heat, stirring constantly with a heatproof spatula or wooden spoon, until the custard thickens slightly and coats the back of the spatula (about 5-7 minutes). Do not let it boil.
5. **Combine Lemon and Cream Mixtures:**
    - Gradually whisk the warm lemon juice mixture into the custard until well combined.
6. **Chill:**
    - Remove from heat and stir in the vanilla extract. Strain the mixture through a fine-mesh sieve into a clean bowl to remove the lemon zest and any bits

of cooked egg. Place the bowl in an ice bath or refrigerator until completely chilled, stirring occasionally.
7. **Churn:**
   - Once chilled, pour the lemon custard into an ice cream maker and churn according to the manufacturer's instructions until it reaches a soft-serve consistency.
8. **Freeze:**
   - Transfer the churned lemon ice cream into an airtight container, pressing a piece of parchment paper directly against the surface to prevent ice crystals from forming. Freeze for at least 4 hours or until firm.
9. **Serve:**
   - Scoop and enjoy your creamy and tangy Lemon Ice Cream! It's a delightful dessert with a refreshing citrus flavor that's perfect for a sunny day.

Orange Ice Cream

Ingredients:

- 1 cup freshly squeezed orange juice (about 4-5 oranges)
- Zest of 2 oranges
- 1 1/2 cups granulated sugar
- 2 cups heavy cream
- 1 cup whole milk
- Pinch of salt
- 6 large egg yolks
- 1 teaspoon vanilla extract

Instructions:

1. **Prepare the Orange Base:**
   - In a medium saucepan, combine the freshly squeezed orange juice, orange zest, and 1 cup of sugar. Heat over medium heat, stirring occasionally, until the sugar is dissolved and the mixture is steaming. Remove from heat and let it cool slightly.
2. **Prepare the Cream Mixture:**
   - In another medium saucepan, combine the heavy cream, whole milk, remaining 1/2 cup of sugar, and salt. Heat over medium heat, stirring occasionally, until it begins to steam and small bubbles form around the edges. Do not let it boil.
3. **Temper the Eggs:**
   - In a separate bowl, whisk together the egg yolks until smooth. Gradually whisk in about 1 cup of the warm cream mixture, a little at a time, to temper the eggs.
4. **Combine and Cook:**
   - Pour the tempered egg mixture back into the saucepan with the remaining cream mixture. Cook over medium heat, stirring constantly with a heatproof spatula or wooden spoon, until the custard thickens slightly and coats the back of the spatula (about 5-7 minutes). Do not let it boil.
5. **Combine Orange and Cream Mixtures:**
   - Gradually whisk the warm orange juice mixture into the custard until well combined.
6. **Chill:**
   - Remove from heat and stir in the vanilla extract. Strain the mixture through a fine-mesh sieve into a clean bowl to remove the orange zest and any bits

of cooked egg. Place the bowl in an ice bath or refrigerator until completely chilled, stirring occasionally.

7. **Churn:**
    - Once chilled, pour the orange custard into an ice cream maker and churn according to the manufacturer's instructions until it reaches a soft-serve consistency.
8. **Freeze:**
    - Transfer the churned orange ice cream into an airtight container, pressing a piece of parchment paper directly against the surface to prevent ice crystals from forming. Freeze for at least 4 hours or until firm.
9. **Serve:**
    - Scoop and enjoy your creamy and refreshing Orange Ice Cream! It's a delightful dessert with a vibrant citrus flavor that's perfect for a sunny day or any occasion.

Mango Ice Cream

Ingredients:

- 2 cups ripe mango puree (about 2-3 mangoes)
- 1 cup granulated sugar
- 2 cups heavy cream
- 1 cup whole milk
- Pinch of salt
- 6 large egg yolks
- 1 teaspoon vanilla extract

Instructions:

1. **Prepare the Mango Puree:**
   - Peel and dice the mangoes. Blend the diced mangoes in a blender or food processor until smooth to make the mango puree. Set aside.
2. **Prepare the Base:**
   - In a medium saucepan, combine the heavy cream, whole milk, and half of the sugar (about 1/2 cup). Heat over medium heat, stirring occasionally, until it begins to steam and small bubbles form around the edges. Do not let it boil.
3. **Mix Mango Puree and Sugar:**
   - In a separate bowl, combine the mango puree with the remaining sugar (about 1/2 cup) until the sugar dissolves.
4. **Temper the Eggs:**
   - In another bowl, whisk the egg yolks until smooth. Gradually whisk in about 1 cup of the warm cream mixture, a little at a time, to temper the eggs and prevent curdling.
5. **Combine and Cook:**
   - Pour the tempered egg mixture back into the saucepan with the remaining cream mixture. Cook over medium heat, stirring constantly with a heatproof spatula or wooden spoon, until the custard thickens slightly and coats the back of the spatula (about 5-7 minutes). Do not let it boil.
6. **Combine Mango Puree and Custard:**
   - Gradually whisk the warm custard mixture into the mango puree until well combined.
7. **Chill:**
   - Remove from heat and stir in the vanilla extract. Strain the mixture through a fine-mesh sieve into a clean bowl to remove any bits of cooked egg.

Place the bowl in an ice bath or refrigerator until completely chilled, stirring occasionally.
8. **Churn:**
    - Once chilled, pour the mango custard into an ice cream maker and churn according to the manufacturer's instructions until it reaches a soft-serve consistency.
9. **Freeze:**
    - Transfer the churned mango ice cream into an airtight container, pressing a piece of parchment paper directly against the surface to prevent ice crystals from forming. Freeze for at least 4 hours or until firm.
10. **Serve:**
    - Scoop and enjoy your creamy and tropical Mango Ice Cream! It's a delightful dessert with the natural sweetness and flavor of fresh mangoes, perfect for enjoying on its own or as part of a fruit sundae.

Pineapple Ice Cream

Ingredients:

- 2 cups fresh pineapple puree (about 1 small pineapple)
- 1 cup granulated sugar
- 2 cups heavy cream
- 1 cup whole milk
- Pinch of salt
- 6 large egg yolks
- 1 teaspoon vanilla extract

Instructions:

1. **Prepare the Pineapple Puree:**
    - Peel and core the pineapple, then cut it into chunks. Blend the pineapple chunks in a blender or food processor until smooth to make the pineapple puree. Set aside.
2. **Prepare the Base:**
    - In a medium saucepan, combine the heavy cream, whole milk, and half of the sugar (about 1/2 cup). Heat over medium heat, stirring occasionally, until it begins to steam and small bubbles form around the edges. Do not let it boil.
3. **Mix Pineapple Puree and Sugar:**
    - In a separate bowl, combine the pineapple puree with the remaining sugar (about 1/2 cup) until the sugar dissolves.
4. **Temper the Eggs:**
    - In another bowl, whisk the egg yolks until smooth. Gradually whisk in about 1 cup of the warm cream mixture, a little at a time, to temper the eggs and prevent curdling.
5. **Combine and Cook:**
    - Pour the tempered egg mixture back into the saucepan with the remaining cream mixture. Cook over medium heat, stirring constantly with a heatproof spatula or wooden spoon, until the custard thickens slightly and coats the back of the spatula (about 5-7 minutes). Do not let it boil.
6. **Combine Pineapple Puree and Custard:**
    - Gradually whisk the warm custard mixture into the pineapple puree until well combined.
7. **Chill:**

- Remove from heat and stir in the vanilla extract. Strain the mixture through a fine-mesh sieve into a clean bowl to remove any bits of cooked egg. Place the bowl in an ice bath or refrigerator until completely chilled, stirring occasionally.

8. **Churn:**
   - Once chilled, pour the pineapple custard into an ice cream maker and churn according to the manufacturer's instructions until it reaches a soft-serve consistency.

9. **Freeze:**
   - Transfer the churned pineapple ice cream into an airtight container, pressing a piece of parchment paper directly against the surface to prevent ice crystals from forming. Freeze for at least 4 hours or until firm.

10. **Serve:**
    - Scoop and enjoy your creamy and tropical Pineapple Ice Cream! It's a delightful dessert with the bright and sweet flavor of fresh pineapple, perfect for enjoying on its own or with other tropical fruits.

Coconut Ice Cream

Ingredients:

- 1 can (13.5 oz) coconut milk (full fat)
- 1 can (13.5 oz) coconut cream
- 1 cup heavy cream
- 3/4 cup granulated sugar
- Pinch of salt
- 1 teaspoon vanilla extract
- Optional: 1/2 cup shredded coconut (sweetened or unsweetened), toasted

Instructions:

1. **Prepare the Base:**
    - In a medium saucepan, combine the coconut milk, coconut cream, heavy cream, half of the sugar (about 6 tablespoons), and salt. Heat over medium heat, stirring occasionally, until it begins to steam and small bubbles form around the edges. Do not let it boil.
2. **Infuse and Sweeten:**
    - If using shredded coconut, add it to the mixture to infuse the coconut flavor. Let it steep for about 10-15 minutes off the heat. Then, strain the mixture through a fine-mesh sieve into a clean bowl to remove the shredded coconut. Press down on the coconut solids to extract all the liquid. Discard the solids.
3. **Prepare the Custard:**
    - In a separate bowl, whisk together the egg yolks and the remaining sugar until well combined and slightly thickened.
4. **Temper and Cook the Custard:**
    - Gradually pour the warm coconut-infused cream mixture into the bowl with the egg yolks and sugar, whisking constantly, to temper the eggs. Pour the mixture back into the saucepan.
5. **Cook the Custard:**
    - Cook the custard mixture over medium heat, stirring constantly with a wooden spoon or heatproof spatula, until it thickens slightly and coats the back of the spoon (about 5-7 minutes). Do not let it boil.
6. **Chill:**
    - Remove from heat and stir in the vanilla extract. Strain the custard through a fine-mesh sieve into a clean bowl to ensure smooth texture. Place the

bowl in an ice bath or refrigerate until completely chilled, stirring occasionally.

7. **Churn:**
   - Once chilled, pour the coconut custard into an ice cream maker and churn according to the manufacturer's instructions until it reaches a soft-serve consistency.

8. **Optional: Toasted Coconut:**
   - If you want to add texture, sprinkle toasted shredded coconut on top of the churned ice cream during the last few minutes of churning.

9. **Freeze:**
   - Transfer the churned coconut ice cream into an airtight container, pressing a piece of parchment paper directly against the surface to prevent ice crystals from forming. Freeze for at least 4 hours or until firm.

10. **Serve:**
    - Scoop and enjoy your creamy and tropical Coconut Ice Cream! It's perfect on its own or as a topping for desserts like pineapple upside-down cake or alongside fresh tropical fruits.

Black Forest Ice Cream (with cherries and chocolate)

Ingredients:

- 1 cup pitted cherries, chopped
- 1/2 cup granulated sugar
- 1 tablespoon lemon juice
- 2 cups heavy cream
- 1 cup whole milk
- 3/4 cup granulated sugar
- Pinch of salt
- 6 large egg yolks
- 1 teaspoon vanilla extract
- 1/2 cup dark chocolate, chopped or chocolate chips

Instructions:

1. **Prepare the Cherries:**
   - In a small saucepan, combine the chopped cherries, 1/2 cup sugar, and lemon juice. Cook over medium heat, stirring occasionally, until the cherries release their juices and the mixture thickens slightly (about 5-7 minutes). Remove from heat and let it cool completely.
2. **Prepare the Base:**
   - In a medium saucepan, combine the heavy cream, whole milk, remaining 3/4 cup sugar, and salt. Heat over medium heat, stirring occasionally, until it begins to steam and small bubbles form around the edges. Do not let it boil.
3. **Prepare the Custard:**
   - In a separate bowl, whisk together the egg yolks until smooth. Gradually whisk in about 1 cup of the warm cream mixture, a little at a time, to temper the eggs and prevent curdling.
4. **Combine and Cook:**
   - Pour the tempered egg mixture back into the saucepan with the remaining cream mixture. Cook over medium heat, stirring constantly with a heatproof spatula or wooden spoon, until the custard thickens slightly and coats the back of the spatula (about 5-7 minutes). Do not let it boil.
5. **Flavor the Base:**
   - Remove from heat and stir in the vanilla extract. Allow the custard to cool slightly.
6. **Assemble the Ice Cream:**

- Stir the cooled cherry mixture and chopped dark chocolate into the custard until well combined.
7. **Chill:**
    - Strain the mixture through a fine-mesh sieve into a clean bowl to ensure smooth texture. Place the bowl in an ice bath or refrigerator until completely chilled, stirring occasionally.
8. **Churn:**
    - Once chilled, pour the Black Forest custard into an ice cream maker and churn according to the manufacturer's instructions until it reaches a soft-serve consistency.
9. **Freeze:**
    - Transfer the churned Black Forest ice cream into an airtight container, pressing a piece of parchment paper directly against the surface to prevent ice crystals from forming. Freeze for at least 4 hours or until firm.
10. **Serve:**
    - Scoop and enjoy your indulgent Black Forest Ice Cream! It's a delightful dessert that combines the flavors of cherries and chocolate in a creamy, frozen treat reminiscent of the classic cake.

Tiramisu Ice Cream

Ingredients:

- 1 cup mascarpone cheese
- 1 cup heavy cream
- 1 cup whole milk
- 3/4 cup granulated sugar
- 4 large egg yolks
- 1/4 cup brewed espresso or strong coffee, cooled
- 2 tablespoons coffee liqueur (optional)
- 1 teaspoon vanilla extract
- 1/4 cup cocoa powder
- Ladyfinger biscuits, chopped (optional, for texture)

Instructions:

1. **Prepare the Base:**
   - In a medium saucepan, combine the heavy cream, whole milk, and half of the sugar (about 6 tablespoons). Heat over medium heat, stirring occasionally, until it begins to steam and small bubbles form around the edges. Do not let it boil.
2. **Mix Mascarpone and Coffee:**
   - In a separate bowl, whisk together the mascarpone cheese, brewed espresso or coffee, coffee liqueur (if using), and vanilla extract until smooth.
3. **Temper the Eggs:**
   - In another bowl, whisk the egg yolks with the remaining sugar (about 6 tablespoons) until smooth.
4. **Combine and Cook:**
   - Gradually whisk in about 1 cup of the warm cream mixture into the egg yolks, a little at a time, to temper the eggs. Pour the tempered egg mixture back into the saucepan with the remaining cream mixture.
5. **Cook the Custard:**
   - Cook the custard mixture over medium heat, stirring constantly with a heatproof spatula or wooden spoon, until it thickens slightly and coats the back of the spatula (about 5-7 minutes). Do not let it boil.
6. **Combine Mascarpone Mixture and Custard:**
   - Remove from heat and whisk in the mascarpone mixture until smooth and well combined.

7. **Chill:**
   - Strain the mixture through a fine-mesh sieve into a clean bowl to ensure smooth texture. Place the bowl in an ice bath or refrigerator until completely chilled, stirring occasionally.
8. **Churn:**
   - Once chilled, pour the Tiramisu custard into an ice cream maker and churn according to the manufacturer's instructions until it reaches a soft-serve consistency.
9. **Add Cocoa Powder:**
   - During the last few minutes of churning, gradually add the cocoa powder into the ice cream maker, allowing it to mix evenly.
10. **Optional: Add Ladyfinger Biscuits:**
    - If desired, fold in chopped ladyfinger biscuits into the churned ice cream for added texture and flavor reminiscent of Tiramisu.
11. **Freeze:**
    - Transfer the churned Tiramisu ice cream into an airtight container, pressing a piece of parchment paper directly against the surface to prevent ice crystals from forming. Freeze for at least 4 hours or until firm.
12. **Serve:**
    - Scoop and enjoy your creamy and decadent Tiramisu Ice Cream! It's a delightful frozen twist on the classic Italian dessert, perfect for coffee and dessert lovers alike.

Caramel Ice Cream

Ingredients:

- 1 cup granulated sugar
- 2 cups heavy cream
- 1 cup whole milk
- Pinch of salt
- 6 large egg yolks
- 1 teaspoon vanilla extract

Instructions:

1. **Prepare the Caramel:**
    - In a heavy-bottomed saucepan, heat the granulated sugar over medium heat. Stir constantly with a heatproof spatula or wooden spoon until the sugar melts and turns into a smooth amber-colored liquid. Be careful not to burn the sugar.
2. **Warm the Cream Mixture:**
    - In another medium saucepan, combine the heavy cream, whole milk, and salt. Heat over medium heat until it begins to steam and small bubbles form around the edges. Do not let it boil.
3. **Combine Caramel and Cream:**
    - Once the caramel is ready (smooth and amber-colored), carefully pour the warm cream mixture into the caramelized sugar, stirring constantly. The mixture will bubble vigorously, so be cautious of splattering.
4. **Prepare the Custard:**
    - In a separate bowl, whisk together the egg yolks until smooth. Gradually whisk in about 1 cup of the warm caramel cream mixture into the egg yolks, a little at a time, to temper the eggs.
5. **Cook the Custard:**
    - Pour the tempered egg mixture back into the saucepan with the remaining caramel cream mixture. Cook over medium heat, stirring constantly with a heatproof spatula or wooden spoon, until the custard thickens slightly and coats the back of the spatula (about 5-7 minutes). Do not let it boil.
6. **Strain and Chill:**
    - Remove from heat and stir in the vanilla extract. Strain the custard through a fine-mesh sieve into a clean bowl to remove any bits of cooked egg or caramelized sugar. Place the bowl in an ice bath or refrigerator until completely chilled, stirring occasionally.

7. **Churn:**
    - Once chilled, pour the caramel custard into an ice cream maker and churn according to the manufacturer's instructions until it reaches a soft-serve consistency.
8. **Freeze:**
    - Transfer the churned caramel ice cream into an airtight container, pressing a piece of parchment paper directly against the surface to prevent ice crystals from forming. Freeze for at least 4 hours or until firm.
9. **Serve:**
    - Scoop and enjoy your creamy and decadent Caramel Ice Cream! It's perfect on its own, drizzled with extra caramel sauce, or as a delightful addition to desserts like apple pie or brownies.

Salted Caramel Ice Cream

Ingredients:

- 1 cup granulated sugar
- 2 cups heavy cream
- 1 cup whole milk
- Pinch of sea salt (adjust to taste)
- 6 large egg yolks
- 1 teaspoon vanilla extract
- Sea salt flakes, for garnish (optional)

Instructions:

1. **Prepare the Caramel:**
    - In a heavy-bottomed saucepan, heat the granulated sugar over medium heat. Stir constantly with a heatproof spatula or wooden spoon until the sugar melts and turns into a smooth amber-colored liquid. Be careful not to burn the sugar.
2. **Warm the Cream Mixture:**
    - In another medium saucepan, combine the heavy cream, whole milk, and a pinch of sea salt. Heat over medium heat until it begins to steam and small bubbles form around the edges. Do not let it boil.
3. **Combine Caramel and Cream:**
    - Once the caramel is ready (smooth and amber-colored), carefully pour the warm cream mixture into the caramelized sugar, stirring constantly. The mixture will bubble vigorously, so be cautious of splattering.
4. **Prepare the Custard:**
    - In a separate bowl, whisk together the egg yolks until smooth. Gradually whisk in about 1 cup of the warm caramel cream mixture into the egg yolks, a little at a time, to temper the eggs.
5. **Cook the Custard:**
    - Pour the tempered egg mixture back into the saucepan with the remaining caramel cream mixture. Cook over medium heat, stirring constantly with a heatproof spatula or wooden spoon, until the custard thickens slightly and coats the back of the spatula (about 5-7 minutes). Do not let it boil.
6. **Strain and Chill:**
    - Remove from heat and stir in the vanilla extract. Strain the custard through a fine-mesh sieve into a clean bowl to remove any bits of cooked egg or caramelized sugar. Taste and adjust the saltiness if needed. Place the

bowl in an ice bath or refrigerator until completely chilled, stirring occasionally.

7. **Churn:**
   - Once chilled, pour the salted caramel custard into an ice cream maker and churn according to the manufacturer's instructions until it reaches a soft-serve consistency.

8. **Freeze:**
   - Transfer the churned salted caramel ice cream into an airtight container, pressing a piece of parchment paper directly against the surface to prevent ice crystals from forming. Sprinkle with sea salt flakes if desired. Freeze for at least 4 hours or until firm.

9. **Serve:**
   - Scoop and enjoy your creamy and indulgent Salted Caramel Ice Cream! It's delicious on its own, or you can serve it with caramel sauce, whipped cream, or alongside desserts like warm brownies or apple pie.

Cookies and Cream Ice Cream

Ingredients:

- 2 cups heavy cream
- 1 cup whole milk
- 3/4 cup granulated sugar
- Pinch of salt
- 6 large egg yolks
- 1 teaspoon vanilla extract
- 15-20 chocolate sandwich cookies (like Oreo), crushed into small pieces

Instructions:

1. **Prepare the Base:**
    - In a medium saucepan, combine the heavy cream, whole milk, half of the sugar (about 6 tablespoons), and salt. Heat over medium heat, stirring occasionally, until it begins to steam and small bubbles form around the edges. Do not let it boil.
2. **Prepare the Custard:**
    - In a separate bowl, whisk together the egg yolks and the remaining sugar (about 6 tablespoons) until well combined and slightly thickened.
3. **Temper and Cook the Custard:**
    - Gradually whisk in about 1 cup of the warm cream mixture into the egg yolks, a little at a time, to temper the eggs. Pour the tempered egg mixture back into the saucepan with the remaining cream mixture.
    - Cook the custard mixture over medium heat, stirring constantly with a heatproof spatula or wooden spoon, until it thickens slightly and coats the back of the spatula (about 5-7 minutes). Do not let it boil.
4. **Strain and Chill:**
    - Remove from heat and stir in the vanilla extract. Strain the custard through a fine-mesh sieve into a clean bowl to ensure smooth texture. Place the bowl in an ice bath or refrigerator until completely chilled, stirring occasionally.
5. **Churn:**
    - Once chilled, pour the custard into an ice cream maker and churn according to the manufacturer's instructions until it reaches a soft-serve consistency.
6. **Add Cookie Pieces:**

- During the last few minutes of churning, add the crushed cookie pieces into the ice cream maker. Let the machine incorporate the cookies evenly into the ice cream.

7. **Freeze:**
    - Transfer the churned Cookies and Cream ice cream into an airtight container, pressing a piece of parchment paper directly against the surface to prevent ice crystals from forming. Freeze for at least 4 hours or until firm.

8. **Serve:**
    - Scoop and enjoy your creamy and crunchy Cookies and Cream Ice Cream! It's perfect on its own or as a delicious addition to desserts like brownies or waffle cones.

Peanut Butter Ice Cream

Ingredients:

- 1 cup creamy peanut butter
- 1 cup whole milk
- 2 cups heavy cream
- 3/4 cup granulated sugar
- Pinch of salt
- 6 large egg yolks
- 1 teaspoon vanilla extract

Instructions:

1. **Prepare the Base:**
    - In a medium saucepan, combine the heavy cream, whole milk, half of the sugar (about 6 tablespoons), and salt. Heat over medium heat, stirring occasionally, until it begins to steam and small bubbles form around the edges. Do not let it boil.
2. **Mix Peanut Butter:**
    - In a separate microwave-safe bowl, heat the peanut butter in the microwave for about 30 seconds to soften it slightly.
3. **Prepare the Custard:**
    - In a separate bowl, whisk together the egg yolks and the remaining sugar (about 6 tablespoons) until well combined and slightly thickened.
4. **Temper and Cook the Custard:**
    - Gradually whisk in about 1 cup of the warm cream mixture into the egg yolks, a little at a time, to temper the eggs. Pour the tempered egg mixture back into the saucepan with the remaining cream mixture.
    - Cook the custard mixture over medium heat, stirring constantly with a heatproof spatula or wooden spoon, until it thickens slightly and coats the back of the spatula (about 5-7 minutes). Do not let it boil.
5. **Combine with Peanut Butter:**
    - Remove from heat and whisk in the softened peanut butter until smooth and well combined.
6. **Strain and Chill:**
    - Strain the peanut butter custard through a fine-mesh sieve into a clean bowl to ensure smooth texture. Stir in the vanilla extract. Place the bowl in an ice bath or refrigerator until completely chilled, stirring occasionally.
7. **Churn:**

- Once chilled, pour the peanut butter custard into an ice cream maker and churn according to the manufacturer's instructions until it reaches a soft-serve consistency.
8. **Freeze:**
    - Transfer the churned Peanut Butter Ice Cream into an airtight container, pressing a piece of parchment paper directly against the surface to prevent ice crystals from forming. Freeze for at least 4 hours or until firm.
9. **Serve:**
    - Scoop and enjoy your creamy and nutty Peanut Butter Ice Cream! It's delicious on its own, or you can drizzle it with chocolate sauce or serve it alongside your favorite desserts.

Nutella Ice Cream

Ingredients:

- 1 cup Nutella or other chocolate hazelnut spread
- 1 cup whole milk
- 2 cups heavy cream
- 3/4 cup granulated sugar
- Pinch of salt
- 6 large egg yolks
- 1 teaspoon vanilla extract

Instructions:

1. **Prepare the Base:**
   - In a medium saucepan, combine the heavy cream, whole milk, half of the sugar (about 6 tablespoons), and salt. Heat over medium heat, stirring occasionally, until it begins to steam and small bubbles form around the edges. Do not let it boil.
2. **Mix Nutella:**
   - In a separate microwave-safe bowl, heat the Nutella in the microwave for about 30 seconds to soften it slightly.
3. **Prepare the Custard:**
   - In a separate bowl, whisk together the egg yolks and the remaining sugar (about 6 tablespoons) until well combined and slightly thickened.
4. **Temper and Cook the Custard:**
   - Gradually whisk in about 1 cup of the warm cream mixture into the egg yolks, a little at a time, to temper the eggs. Pour the tempered egg mixture back into the saucepan with the remaining cream mixture.
   - Cook the custard mixture over medium heat, stirring constantly with a heatproof spatula or wooden spoon, until it thickens slightly and coats the back of the spatula (about 5-7 minutes). Do not let it boil.
5. **Combine with Nutella:**
   - Remove from heat and whisk in the softened Nutella until smooth and well combined.
6. **Strain and Chill:**
   - Strain the Nutella custard through a fine-mesh sieve into a clean bowl to ensure smooth texture. Stir in the vanilla extract. Place the bowl in an ice bath or refrigerator until completely chilled, stirring occasionally.
7. **Churn:**

- Once chilled, pour the Nutella custard into an ice cream maker and churn according to the manufacturer's instructions until it reaches a soft-serve consistency.
8. **Freeze:**
    - Transfer the churned Nutella Ice Cream into an airtight container, pressing a piece of parchment paper directly against the surface to prevent ice crystals from forming. Freeze for at least 4 hours or until firm.
9. **Serve:**
    - Scoop and enjoy your creamy and decadent Nutella Ice Cream! It's perfect on its own, or you can drizzle it with chocolate sauce, sprinkle with chopped hazelnuts, or serve it with waffles or crepes.

Stracciatella Ice Cream

Ingredients:

- 2 cups heavy cream
- 1 cup whole milk
- 3/4 cup granulated sugar
- Pinch of salt
- 6 large egg yolks
- 1 teaspoon vanilla extract
- 3 ounces dark chocolate, chopped or chips

Instructions:

1. **Prepare the Base:**
   - In a medium saucepan, combine the heavy cream, whole milk, half of the sugar (about 6 tablespoons), and salt. Heat over medium heat, stirring occasionally, until it begins to steam and small bubbles form around the edges. Do not let it boil.
2. **Prepare the Custard:**
   - In a separate bowl, whisk together the egg yolks and the remaining sugar (about 6 tablespoons) until well combined and slightly thickened.
3. **Temper and Cook the Custard:**
   - Gradually whisk in about 1 cup of the warm cream mixture into the egg yolks, a little at a time, to temper the eggs. Pour the tempered egg mixture back into the saucepan with the remaining cream mixture.
   - Cook the custard mixture over medium heat, stirring constantly with a heatproof spatula or wooden spoon, until it thickens slightly and coats the back of the spatula (about 5-7 minutes). Do not let it boil.
4. **Strain and Chill:**
   - Remove from heat and stir in the vanilla extract. Strain the custard through a fine-mesh sieve into a clean bowl to ensure smooth texture. Place the bowl in an ice bath or refrigerator until completely chilled, stirring occasionally.
5. **Churn:**
   - Once chilled, pour the vanilla custard into an ice cream maker and churn according to the manufacturer's instructions until it reaches a soft-serve consistency.
6. **Prepare the Chocolate Shards:**

- While the ice cream is churning, melt the dark chocolate in a microwave-safe bowl in short intervals, stirring in between until smooth. Let it cool slightly.

7. **Add Chocolate Shards:**
   - During the last few minutes of churning, drizzle the melted chocolate into the ice cream maker in a slow, steady stream. The chocolate will harden upon contact with the cold ice cream, forming delicate shards.

8. **Freeze:**
   - Transfer the churned Stracciatella Ice Cream into an airtight container, pressing a piece of parchment paper directly against the surface to prevent ice crystals from forming. Freeze for at least 4 hours or until firm.

9. **Serve:**
   - Scoop and enjoy your creamy and chocolatey Stracciatella Ice Cream! It's a delightful dessert on its own, or you can serve it with fresh berries, wafers, or as a complement to Italian pastries like cannoli.

White Chocolate Raspberry Ice Cream

Ingredients:

- 1 cup whole milk
- 2 cups heavy cream
- 3/4 cup granulated sugar
- Pinch of salt
- 6 large egg yolks
- 8 ounces white chocolate, finely chopped
- 1 teaspoon vanilla extract
- 1 cup fresh or frozen raspberries, chopped

Instructions:

1. **Prepare the Base:**
   - In a medium saucepan, combine the heavy cream, whole milk, half of the sugar (about 6 tablespoons), and salt. Heat over medium heat, stirring occasionally, until it begins to steam and small bubbles form around the edges. Do not let it boil.
2. **Melt White Chocolate:**
   - Place the finely chopped white chocolate in a heatproof bowl. In a separate saucepan or in the microwave, heat a small amount of the cream mixture until steaming (but not boiling). Pour the hot cream over the white chocolate and let it sit for a minute. Stir until the chocolate is completely melted and smooth. Set aside.
3. **Prepare the Custard:**
   - In a separate bowl, whisk together the egg yolks and the remaining sugar (about 6 tablespoons) until well combined and slightly thickened.
4. **Temper and Cook the Custard:**
   - Gradually whisk in about 1 cup of the warm cream mixture into the egg yolks, a little at a time, to temper the eggs. Pour the tempered egg mixture back into the saucepan with the remaining cream mixture.
   - Cook the custard mixture over medium heat, stirring constantly with a heatproof spatula or wooden spoon, until it thickens slightly and coats the back of the spatula (about 5-7 minutes). Do not let it boil.
5. **Combine with White Chocolate:**
   - Remove from heat and whisk in the melted white chocolate mixture until smooth and well combined. Stir in the vanilla extract.
6. **Strain and Chill:**

- Strain the custard through a fine-mesh sieve into a clean bowl to ensure smooth texture. Place the bowl in an ice bath or refrigerator until completely chilled, stirring occasionally.
7. **Churn:**
    - Once chilled, pour the white chocolate custard into an ice cream maker and churn according to the manufacturer's instructions until it reaches a soft-serve consistency.
8. **Add Raspberries:**
    - During the last few minutes of churning, add the chopped raspberries into the ice cream maker. Let the machine incorporate the raspberries evenly into the ice cream.
9. **Freeze:**
    - Transfer the churned White Chocolate Raspberry Ice Cream into an airtight container, pressing a piece of parchment paper directly against the surface to prevent ice crystals from forming. Freeze for at least 4 hours or until firm.
10. **Serve:**
    - Scoop and enjoy your creamy and fruity White Chocolate Raspberry Ice Cream! It's perfect on its own, or you can garnish it with additional raspberries or a drizzle of melted white chocolate for an extra special treat.

Matcha Green Tea Ice Cream

Ingredients:

- 1 cup whole milk
- 2 cups heavy cream
- 3/4 cup granulated sugar
- Pinch of salt
- 6 large egg yolks
- 3 tablespoons matcha green tea powder
- 1 teaspoon vanilla extract

Instructions:

1. **Prepare the Base:**
    - In a medium saucepan, combine the heavy cream, whole milk, half of the sugar (about 6 tablespoons), and salt. Heat over medium heat, stirring occasionally, until it begins to steam and small bubbles form around the edges. Do not let it boil.
2. **Mix Matcha Green Tea:**
    - In a small bowl, whisk the matcha green tea powder with a small amount of the warm milk until smooth and no lumps remain.
3. **Prepare the Custard:**
    - In a separate bowl, whisk together the egg yolks and the remaining sugar (about 6 tablespoons) until well combined and slightly thickened.
4. **Temper and Cook the Custard:**
    - Gradually whisk in about 1 cup of the warm cream mixture into the egg yolks, a little at a time, to temper the eggs. Pour the tempered egg mixture back into the saucepan with the remaining cream mixture.
    - Cook the custard mixture over medium heat, stirring constantly with a heatproof spatula or wooden spoon, until it thickens slightly and coats the back of the spatula (about 5-7 minutes). Do not let it boil.
5. **Combine with Matcha Mixture:**
    - Remove from heat and whisk in the matcha green tea mixture until well combined and smooth. Stir in the vanilla extract.
6. **Strain and Chill:**
    - Strain the custard through a fine-mesh sieve into a clean bowl to ensure smooth texture. Place the bowl in an ice bath or refrigerator until completely chilled, stirring occasionally.
7. **Churn:**

    - Once chilled, pour the matcha green tea custard into an ice cream maker and churn according to the manufacturer's instructions until it reaches a soft-serve consistency.
8. **Freeze:**
    - Transfer the churned Matcha Green Tea Ice Cream into an airtight container, pressing a piece of parchment paper directly against the surface to prevent ice crystals from forming. Freeze for at least 4 hours or until firm.
9. **Serve:**
    - Scoop and enjoy your creamy and fragrant Matcha Green Tea Ice Cream! It's a wonderful dessert on its own, or you can serve it with a drizzle of honey or alongside Japanese sweets like mochi or red bean paste desserts.

Elderflower Ice Cream

Ingredients:

- 1 cup whole milk
- 2 cups heavy cream
- 3/4 cup granulated sugar
- Pinch of salt
- 6 large egg yolks
- 1/2 cup elderflower cordial or syrup
- 1 teaspoon vanilla extract

Instructions:

1. **Prepare the Base:**
    - In a medium saucepan, combine the heavy cream, whole milk, half of the sugar (about 6 tablespoons), and salt. Heat over medium heat, stirring occasionally, until it begins to steam and small bubbles form around the edges. Do not let it boil.
2. **Mix Elderflower Cordial:**
    - In a small bowl, mix the elderflower cordial or syrup with a small amount of the warm milk until well combined.
3. **Prepare the Custard:**
    - In a separate bowl, whisk together the egg yolks and the remaining sugar (about 6 tablespoons) until well combined and slightly thickened.
4. **Temper and Cook the Custard:**
    - Gradually whisk in about 1 cup of the warm cream mixture into the egg yolks, a little at a time, to temper the eggs. Pour the tempered egg mixture back into the saucepan with the remaining cream mixture.
    - Cook the custard mixture over medium heat, stirring constantly with a heatproof spatula or wooden spoon, until it thickens slightly and coats the back of the spatula (about 5-7 minutes). Do not let it boil.
5. **Combine with Elderflower Mixture:**
    - Remove from heat and whisk in the elderflower mixture until well combined and smooth. Stir in the vanilla extract.
6. **Strain and Chill:**
    - Strain the custard through a fine-mesh sieve into a clean bowl to ensure smooth texture. Place the bowl in an ice bath or refrigerator until completely chilled, stirring occasionally.
7. **Churn:**

- Once chilled, pour the elderflower custard into an ice cream maker and churn according to the manufacturer's instructions until it reaches a soft-serve consistency.

8. **Freeze:**
    - Transfer the churned Elderflower Ice Cream into an airtight container, pressing a piece of parchment paper directly against the surface to prevent ice crystals from forming. Freeze for at least 4 hours or until firm.
9. **Serve:**
    - Scoop and enjoy your delicate and floral Elderflower Ice Cream! It's a lovely dessert on its own, or you can serve it with fresh berries, shortbread cookies, or alongside a slice of lemon cake for a refreshing treat.

Rose Ice Cream

Ingredients:

- 1 cup whole milk
- 2 cups heavy cream
- 3/4 cup granulated sugar
- Pinch of salt
- 6 large egg yolks
- 2-3 tablespoons rose water (adjust to taste)
- Pink food coloring (optional, for color)
- Edible rose petals, for garnish (optional)

Instructions:

1. **Prepare the Base:**
    - In a medium saucepan, combine the heavy cream, whole milk, half of the sugar (about 6 tablespoons), and salt. Heat over medium heat, stirring occasionally, until it begins to steam and small bubbles form around the edges. Do not let it boil.
2. **Mix Rose Water:**
    - In a small bowl, mix the rose water with a small amount of the warm milk until well combined. Adjust the amount of rose water to your preference for a subtle or stronger rose flavor.
3. **Prepare the Custard:**
    - In a separate bowl, whisk together the egg yolks and the remaining sugar (about 6 tablespoons) until well combined and slightly thickened.
4. **Temper and Cook the Custard:**
    - Gradually whisk in about 1 cup of the warm cream mixture into the egg yolks, a little at a time, to temper the eggs. Pour the tempered egg mixture back into the saucepan with the remaining cream mixture.
    - Cook the custard mixture over medium heat, stirring constantly with a heatproof spatula or wooden spoon, until it thickens slightly and coats the back of the spatula (about 5-7 minutes). Do not let it boil.
5. **Add Rose Water and Coloring:**
    - Remove from heat and whisk in the rose water mixture until well combined. Add a few drops of pink food coloring, if desired, to achieve a pale pink color. Stir until evenly distributed.
6. **Strain and Chill:**

- Strain the custard through a fine-mesh sieve into a clean bowl to ensure smooth texture. Place the bowl in an ice bath or refrigerator until completely chilled, stirring occasionally.
7. **Churn:**
    - Once chilled, pour the rose custard into an ice cream maker and churn according to the manufacturer's instructions until it reaches a soft-serve consistency.
8. **Freeze:**
    - Transfer the churned Rose Ice Cream into an airtight container, pressing a piece of parchment paper directly against the surface to prevent ice crystals from forming. Freeze for at least 4 hours or until firm.
9. **Serve:**
    - Scoop and enjoy your delicately floral Rose Ice Cream! Serve it garnished with edible rose petals for a beautiful presentation. It pairs wonderfully with shortbread cookies, fresh fruit, or as a unique topping for desserts like pavlova or sponge cake.

Lavender Honey Ice Cream

Ingredients:

- 1 cup whole milk
- 2 cups heavy cream
- 3/4 cup granulated sugar
- Pinch of salt
- 6 large egg yolks
- 2 tablespoons dried culinary lavender buds
- 1/3 cup honey
- 1 teaspoon vanilla extract

Instructions:

1. **Infuse Milk with Lavender:**
   - In a medium saucepan, combine the whole milk and heavy cream. Add the dried lavender buds to the mixture. Heat over medium heat, stirring occasionally, until it begins to steam and small bubbles form around the edges. Do not let it boil. Remove from heat and let the lavender steep in the milk mixture for about 20-30 minutes to infuse the flavors. Strain out the lavender buds and discard.
2. **Prepare the Custard:**
   - In a separate bowl, whisk together the egg yolks and the sugar until well combined and slightly thickened.
3. **Temper and Cook the Custard:**
   - Gradually whisk in about 1 cup of the infused cream mixture into the egg yolks, a little at a time, to temper the eggs. Pour the tempered egg mixture back into the saucepan with the remaining infused cream mixture.
   - Cook the custard mixture over medium heat, stirring constantly with a heatproof spatula or wooden spoon, until it thickens slightly and coats the back of the spatula (about 5-7 minutes). Do not let it boil.
4. **Add Honey and Vanilla:**
   - Remove from heat and whisk in the honey and vanilla extract until well combined.
5. **Strain and Chill:**
   - Strain the custard through a fine-mesh sieve into a clean bowl to remove any cooked egg bits and ensure a smooth texture. Place the bowl in an ice bath or refrigerator until completely chilled, stirring occasionally.
6. **Churn:**

- Once chilled, pour the lavender honey custard into an ice cream maker and churn according to the manufacturer's instructions until it reaches a soft-serve consistency.

7. **Freeze:**
   - Transfer the churned Lavender Honey Ice Cream into an airtight container, pressing a piece of parchment paper directly against the surface to prevent ice crystals from forming. Freeze for at least 4 hours or until firm.

8. **Serve:**
   - Scoop and enjoy your fragrant and sweet Lavender Honey Ice Cream! It's delightful on its own, or you can serve it with a drizzle of additional honey or alongside lavender shortbread cookies for a beautiful and aromatic dessert experience.

Apple Pie Ice Cream

Ingredients:

- 2 cups heavy cream
- 1 cup whole milk
- 3/4 cup granulated sugar
- Pinch of salt
- 6 large egg yolks
- 1 teaspoon vanilla extract
- 1 teaspoon ground cinnamon
- 1/4 teaspoon ground nutmeg
- 2 cups chopped apple pie filling (homemade or store-bought)
- 1 cup crushed graham crackers or pie crust pieces (optional, for texture)

Instructions:

1. **Prepare the Base:**
   - In a medium saucepan, combine the heavy cream, whole milk, half of the sugar (about 6 tablespoons), salt, vanilla extract, ground cinnamon, and ground nutmeg. Heat over medium heat, stirring occasionally, until it begins to steam and small bubbles form around the edges. Do not let it boil.
2. **Prepare the Custard:**
   - In a separate bowl, whisk together the egg yolks and the remaining sugar (about 6 tablespoons) until well combined and slightly thickened.
3. **Temper and Cook the Custard:**
   - Gradually whisk in about 1 cup of the warm cream mixture into the egg yolks, a little at a time, to temper the eggs. Pour the tempered egg mixture back into the saucepan with the remaining cream mixture.
   - Cook the custard mixture over medium heat, stirring constantly with a heatproof spatula or wooden spoon, until it thickens slightly and coats the back of the spatula (about 5-7 minutes). Do not let it boil.
4. **Add Apple Pie Filling:**
   - Remove from heat and stir in the chopped apple pie filling. Make sure the apples are evenly distributed throughout the custard.
5. **Optional: Add Pie Crust Pieces:**
   - If desired, fold in crushed graham crackers or pieces of pie crust for added texture and to mimic the crust of an apple pie.
6. **Strain and Chill:**

- Strain the custard through a fine-mesh sieve into a clean bowl to ensure smooth texture and remove any lumps. Place the bowl in an ice bath or refrigerator until completely chilled, stirring occasionally.

7. **Churn:**
    - Once chilled, pour the apple pie custard into an ice cream maker and churn according to the manufacturer's instructions until it reaches a soft-serve consistency.
8. **Freeze:**
    - Transfer the churned Apple Pie Ice Cream into an airtight container, pressing a piece of parchment paper directly against the surface to prevent ice crystals from forming. Freeze for at least 4 hours or until firm.
9. **Serve:**
    - Scoop and enjoy your delicious Apple Pie Ice Cream! Serve it on its own or with a sprinkle of cinnamon or a drizzle of caramel sauce for an extra indulgent treat that captures the flavors of apple pie in every bite.

Cheesecake Ice Cream

Ingredients:

- 2 cups heavy cream
- 1 cup whole milk
- 3/4 cup granulated sugar
- Pinch of salt
- 6 large egg yolks
- 8 ounces cream cheese, softened
- 1 teaspoon vanilla extract
- 1 cup graham cracker crumbs
- 1/2 cup strawberry or raspberry jam (optional, for swirls)

Instructions:

1. **Prepare the Base:**
    - In a medium saucepan, combine the heavy cream, whole milk, half of the sugar (about 6 tablespoons), and salt. Heat over medium heat, stirring occasionally, until it begins to steam and small bubbles form around the edges. Do not let it boil.
2. **Prepare the Cream Cheese Mixture:**
    - In a separate bowl, beat the softened cream cheese until smooth and creamy. Gradually add the remaining sugar (about 6 tablespoons) and beat until well combined.
3. **Temper and Cook the Custard:**
    - In another bowl, whisk the egg yolks until slightly thickened. Gradually whisk in about 1 cup of the warm cream mixture into the egg yolks, a little at a time, to temper the eggs. Pour the tempered egg mixture back into the saucepan with the remaining cream mixture.
    - Cook the custard mixture over medium heat, stirring constantly with a heatproof spatula or wooden spoon, until it thickens slightly and coats the back of the spatula (about 5-7 minutes). Do not let it boil.
4. **Combine Custard with Cream Cheese:**
    - Remove from heat. Gradually whisk the hot custard into the cream cheese mixture until smooth and well combined. Stir in the vanilla extract.
5. **Chill:**
    - Strain the custard through a fine-mesh sieve into a clean bowl to ensure smooth texture. Cover the bowl with plastic wrap, pressing it directly onto

the surface of the custard to prevent a skin from forming. Chill in the refrigerator for at least 4 hours or overnight until completely cold.
6. **Churn:**
   - Once chilled, pour the custard into an ice cream maker and churn according to the manufacturer's instructions until it reaches a soft-serve consistency.
7. **Add Graham Cracker Crumbs:**
   - During the last few minutes of churning, add the graham cracker crumbs to the ice cream maker. Let it mix until evenly distributed.
8. **Optional: Add Fruit Swirls:**
   - If desired, swirl in strawberry or raspberry jam into the ice cream during the last few minutes of churning for a fruity addition.
9. **Freeze:**
   - Transfer the churned Cheesecake Ice Cream into an airtight container, layering with additional graham cracker crumbs and swirls of jam, if desired. Press a piece of parchment paper directly against the surface of the ice cream to prevent ice crystals from forming. Freeze for at least 4 hours or until firm.
10. **Serve:**
    - Scoop and enjoy your creamy and indulgent Cheesecake Ice Cream! Serve it with fresh berries, extra graham cracker crumbs, or a drizzle of caramel sauce for a delicious dessert reminiscent of classic cheesecake.

Red Velvet Ice Cream

Ingredients:

- 2 cups heavy cream
- 1 cup whole milk
- 3/4 cup granulated sugar
- Pinch of salt
- 6 large egg yolks
- 2 teaspoons cocoa powder
- 1 tablespoon red food coloring
- 1 teaspoon vanilla extract
- 4 ounces cream cheese, softened
- 1/2 cup powdered sugar
- 1/2 cup buttermilk
- 1 teaspoon distilled white vinegar

Instructions:

1. **Prepare the Base:**
    - In a medium saucepan, combine the heavy cream, whole milk, half of the granulated sugar (about 6 tablespoons), and salt. Heat over medium heat, stirring occasionally, until it begins to steam and small bubbles form around the edges. Do not let it boil.
2. **Mix Cocoa Powder and Food Coloring:**
    - In a small bowl, whisk together the cocoa powder and red food coloring until smooth. Add this mixture to the cream mixture and stir until well combined. Heat gently until the mixture is warm, stirring constantly. Remove from heat.
3. **Prepare the Custard:**
    - In a separate bowl, whisk together the egg yolks and the remaining granulated sugar (about 6 tablespoons) until well combined and slightly thickened.
4. **Temper and Cook the Custard:**
    - Gradually whisk in about 1 cup of the warm cream mixture into the egg yolks, a little at a time, to temper the eggs. Pour the tempered egg mixture back into the saucepan with the remaining cream mixture.
    - Cook the custard mixture over medium heat, stirring constantly with a heatproof spatula or wooden spoon, until it thickens slightly and coats the back of the spatula (about 5-7 minutes). Do not let it boil.

5. **Combine with Cream Cheese Mixture:**
   - In a separate bowl, beat the softened cream cheese until smooth. Add the powdered sugar and beat until creamy. Gradually add the warm custard mixture to the cream cheese mixture, stirring until smooth and well combined. Stir in the vanilla extract.
6. **Add Buttermilk and Vinegar:**
   - Stir in the buttermilk and distilled white vinegar until fully incorporated. This adds tanginess and helps mimic the flavor profile of red velvet cake.
7. **Chill:**
   - Strain the custard through a fine-mesh sieve into a clean bowl to ensure smooth texture. Cover the bowl with plastic wrap, pressing it directly onto the surface of the custard to prevent a skin from forming. Chill in the refrigerator for at least 4 hours or overnight until completely cold.
8. **Churn:**
   - Once chilled, pour the custard into an ice cream maker and churn according to the manufacturer's instructions until it reaches a soft-serve consistency.
9. **Freeze:**
   - Transfer the churned Red Velvet Ice Cream into an airtight container, pressing a piece of parchment paper directly against the surface of the ice cream to prevent ice crystals from forming. Freeze for at least 4 hours or until firm.
10. **Serve:**
    - Scoop and enjoy your creamy and decadent Red Velvet Ice Cream! Serve it with chocolate sauce, whipped cream, or extra red velvet cake crumbs for an indulgent dessert that captures the flavors of red velvet cake in a frozen treat.

Banana Nut Ice Cream

Ingredients:

- 2 cups heavy cream
- 1 cup whole milk
- 3/4 cup granulated sugar
- Pinch of salt
- 6 large egg yolks
- 4 ripe bananas, mashed
- 1 teaspoon vanilla extract
- 1 cup chopped toasted nuts (such as walnuts or pecans)

Instructions:

1. **Prepare the Base:**
    - In a medium saucepan, combine the heavy cream, whole milk, half of the sugar (about 6 tablespoons), and salt. Heat over medium heat, stirring occasionally, until it begins to steam and small bubbles form around the edges. Do not let it boil.
2. **Prepare the Custard:**
    - In a separate bowl, whisk together the egg yolks and the remaining sugar (about 6 tablespoons) until well combined and slightly thickened.
3. **Temper and Cook the Custard:**
    - Gradually whisk in about 1 cup of the warm cream mixture into the egg yolks, a little at a time, to temper the eggs. Pour the tempered egg mixture back into the saucepan with the remaining cream mixture.
    - Cook the custard mixture over medium heat, stirring constantly with a heatproof spatula or wooden spoon, until it thickens slightly and coats the back of the spatula (about 5-7 minutes). Do not let it boil.
4. **Add Mashed Bananas:**
    - Remove from heat and whisk in the mashed bananas and vanilla extract until well combined.
5. **Chill:**
    - Strain the custard through a fine-mesh sieve into a clean bowl to ensure smooth texture. Cover the bowl with plastic wrap, pressing it directly onto the surface of the custard to prevent a skin from forming. Chill in the refrigerator for at least 4 hours or overnight until completely cold.
6. **Churn:**

- Once chilled, pour the banana custard into an ice cream maker and churn according to the manufacturer's instructions until it reaches a soft-serve consistency.

7. **Add Toasted Nuts:**
   - During the last few minutes of churning, add the chopped toasted nuts to the ice cream maker. Let it mix until evenly distributed.
8. **Freeze:**
   - Transfer the churned Banana Nut Ice Cream into an airtight container, pressing a piece of parchment paper directly against the surface of the ice cream to prevent ice crystals from forming. Freeze for at least 4 hours or until firm.
9. **Serve:**
   - Scoop and enjoy your creamy and nutty Banana Nut Ice Cream! Serve it with extra toasted nuts on top or drizzled with caramel sauce for a delicious dessert that's perfect on its own or as a complement to banana bread or waffles.

Pina Colada Ice Cream

Ingredients:

- 2 cups heavy cream
- 1 cup canned coconut milk (full-fat)
- 3/4 cup granulated sugar
- Pinch of salt
- 6 large egg yolks
- 1 cup crushed pineapple (fresh or canned, drained)
- 1/2 cup sweetened shredded coconut
- 1 teaspoon coconut extract
- 1 teaspoon rum extract (optional, for a hint of rum flavor)
- 1/2 cup toasted coconut flakes (for garnish, optional)

Instructions:

1. **Prepare the Base:**
   - In a medium saucepan, combine the heavy cream, canned coconut milk, half of the sugar (about 6 tablespoons), and salt. Heat over medium heat, stirring occasionally, until it begins to steam and small bubbles form around the edges. Do not let it boil.
2. **Prepare the Custard:**
   - In a separate bowl, whisk together the egg yolks and the remaining sugar (about 6 tablespoons) until well combined and slightly thickened.
3. **Temper and Cook the Custard:**
   - Gradually whisk in about 1 cup of the warm cream mixture into the egg yolks, a little at a time, to temper the eggs. Pour the tempered egg mixture back into the saucepan with the remaining cream mixture.
   - Cook the custard mixture over medium heat, stirring constantly with a heatproof spatula or wooden spoon, until it thickens slightly and coats the back of the spatula (about 5-7 minutes). Do not let it boil.
4. **Add Pineapple and Coconut:**
   - Remove from heat and stir in the crushed pineapple and sweetened shredded coconut until well combined. Stir in the coconut extract and rum extract, if using, for additional flavor.
5. **Chill:**
   - Strain the custard through a fine-mesh sieve into a clean bowl to ensure smooth texture. Cover the bowl with plastic wrap, pressing it directly onto

the surface of the custard to prevent a skin from forming. Chill in the refrigerator for at least 4 hours or overnight until completely cold.
6. **Churn:**
    - Once chilled, pour the pina colada custard into an ice cream maker and churn according to the manufacturer's instructions until it reaches a soft-serve consistency.
7. **Freeze:**
    - Transfer the churned Pina Colada Ice Cream into an airtight container, pressing a piece of parchment paper directly against the surface of the ice cream to prevent ice crystals from forming. Freeze for at least 4 hours or until firm.
8. **Serve:**
    - Scoop and enjoy your tropical Pina Colada Ice Cream! Serve it garnished with toasted coconut flakes for added texture and flavor. It's perfect for a summer treat or as a refreshing dessert any time of the year.

S'mores Ice Cream

Ingredients:

- 2 cups heavy cream
- 1 cup whole milk
- 3/4 cup granulated sugar
- Pinch of salt
- 6 large egg yolks
- 1 teaspoon vanilla extract
- 4 ounces dark chocolate, chopped or chocolate chips
- 1 cup mini marshmallows
- 1 cup crushed graham crackers
- 1/2 cup chocolate fudge sauce (homemade or store-bought)

Instructions:

1. **Prepare the Base:**
   - In a medium saucepan, combine the heavy cream, whole milk, half of the sugar (about 6 tablespoons), and salt. Heat over medium heat, stirring occasionally, until it begins to steam and small bubbles form around the edges. Do not let it boil.
2. **Prepare the Custard:**
   - In a separate bowl, whisk together the egg yolks and the remaining sugar (about 6 tablespoons) until well combined and slightly thickened.
3. **Temper and Cook the Custard:**
   - Gradually whisk in about 1 cup of the warm cream mixture into the egg yolks, a little at a time, to temper the eggs. Pour the tempered egg mixture back into the saucepan with the remaining cream mixture.
   - Cook the custard mixture over medium heat, stirring constantly with a heatproof spatula or wooden spoon, until it thickens slightly and coats the back of the spatula (about 5-7 minutes). Do not let it boil.
4. **Add Chocolate and Vanilla:**
   - Remove from heat and stir in the chopped dark chocolate or chocolate chips until melted and smooth. Stir in the vanilla extract.
5. **Chill:**
   - Strain the custard through a fine-mesh sieve into a clean bowl to ensure smooth texture. Cover the bowl with plastic wrap, pressing it directly onto the surface of the custard to prevent a skin from forming. Chill in the refrigerator for at least 4 hours or overnight until completely cold.

6. **Churn:**
   - Once chilled, pour the chocolate custard into an ice cream maker and churn according to the manufacturer's instructions until it reaches a soft-serve consistency.
7. **Add Mix-ins:**
   - During the last few minutes of churning, add the mini marshmallows and crushed graham crackers to the ice cream maker. Let it mix until evenly distributed.
8. **Swirl with Fudge Sauce:**
   - Layer the churned ice cream in an airtight container, swirling in chocolate fudge sauce between layers. You can also fold the fudge sauce into the ice cream for a marbled effect.
9. **Freeze:**
   - Press a piece of parchment paper directly against the surface of the ice cream to prevent ice crystals from forming. Freeze for at least 4 hours or until firm.
10. **Serve:**
    - Scoop and enjoy your indulgent S'mores Ice Cream! Serve it with extra graham crackers or a drizzle of fudge sauce for a dessert that combines the nostalgic flavors of s'mores in a cool and creamy treat.

Blueberry Cheesecake Ice Cream

Ingredients:

- 2 cups heavy cream
- 1 cup whole milk
- 3/4 cup granulated sugar
- Pinch of salt
- 6 large egg yolks
- 8 ounces cream cheese, softened
- 1 teaspoon vanilla extract
- 1 cup fresh or frozen blueberries
- 1/2 cup blueberry jam or preserves
- 1 cup graham cracker crumbs

Instructions:

1. **Prepare the Base:**
    - In a medium saucepan, combine the heavy cream, whole milk, half of the sugar (about 6 tablespoons), and salt. Heat over medium heat, stirring occasionally, until it begins to steam and small bubbles form around the edges. Do not let it boil.
2. **Prepare the Cream Cheese Mixture:**
    - In a separate bowl, beat the softened cream cheese until smooth and creamy. Gradually add the remaining sugar (about 6 tablespoons) and beat until well combined.
3. **Temper and Cook the Custard:**
    - In another bowl, whisk the egg yolks until slightly thickened. Gradually whisk in about 1 cup of the warm cream mixture into the egg yolks, a little at a time, to temper the eggs. Pour the tempered egg mixture back into the saucepan with the remaining cream mixture.
    - Cook the custard mixture over medium heat, stirring constantly with a heatproof spatula or wooden spoon, until it thickens slightly and coats the back of the spatula (about 5-7 minutes). Do not let it boil.
4. **Combine Custard with Cream Cheese:**
    - Remove from heat. Gradually whisk the hot custard into the cream cheese mixture until smooth and well combined. Stir in the vanilla extract.
5. **Prepare Blueberry Swirl:**
    - In a small saucepan, heat the blueberries and blueberry jam over medium heat until the mixture begins to simmer. Cook for 5-7 minutes, stirring

occasionally, until the blueberries break down and release their juices. Remove from heat and let cool slightly.

6. **Chill:**
   - Strain the custard through a fine-mesh sieve into a clean bowl to ensure smooth texture. Cover the bowl with plastic wrap, pressing it directly onto the surface of the custard to prevent a skin from forming. Chill in the refrigerator for at least 4 hours or overnight until completely cold.

7. **Churn:**
   - Once chilled, pour the cheesecake custard into an ice cream maker and churn according to the manufacturer's instructions until it reaches a soft-serve consistency.

8. **Layer with Blueberry Swirl and Graham Cracker Crumbs:**
   - Layer the churned ice cream in an airtight container, alternating with spoonfuls of the blueberry swirl and graham cracker crumbs. Swirl gently with a spoon or spatula to create ribbons of blueberry throughout the ice cream.

9. **Freeze:**
   - Press a piece of parchment paper directly against the surface of the ice cream to prevent ice crystals from forming. Freeze for at least 4 hours or until firm.

10. **Serve:**
    - Scoop and enjoy your delicious Blueberry Cheesecake Ice Cream! Serve it with extra graham cracker crumbs on top for added texture, or enjoy it on its own for a creamy and fruity dessert that combines the flavors of cheesecake and blueberries.

Gingerbread Ice Cream

Ingredients:

- 2 cups heavy cream
- 1 cup whole milk
- 3/4 cup dark brown sugar, packed
- Pinch of salt
- 6 large egg yolks
- 1 tablespoon ground ginger
- 1 teaspoon ground cinnamon
- 1/4 teaspoon ground cloves
- 1/4 teaspoon ground nutmeg
- 1/4 teaspoon ground allspice
- 1 teaspoon vanilla extract
- 1/4 cup molasses
- 1/2 cup chopped gingerbread cookies (homemade or store-bought)

Instructions:

1. **Prepare the Base:**
    - In a medium saucepan, combine the heavy cream, whole milk, dark brown sugar, and salt. Heat over medium heat, stirring occasionally, until the mixture begins to steam and small bubbles form around the edges. Do not let it boil.
2. **Prepare the Spices:**
    - In a small bowl, mix together the ground ginger, cinnamon, cloves, nutmeg, and allspice until well combined.
3. **Prepare the Custard:**
    - In a separate bowl, whisk together the egg yolks until slightly thickened. Gradually whisk in about 1 cup of the warm cream mixture into the egg yolks, a little at a time, to temper the eggs. Pour the tempered egg mixture back into the saucepan with the remaining cream mixture.
    - Cook the custard mixture over medium heat, stirring constantly with a heatproof spatula or wooden spoon, until it thickens slightly and coats the back of the spatula (about 5-7 minutes). Do not let it boil.
4. **Add Spices, Molasses, and Vanilla:**
    - Remove from heat and whisk in the mixed spices, molasses, and vanilla extract until well combined. Taste and adjust spices if desired.
5. **Chill:**

- Strain the custard through a fine-mesh sieve into a clean bowl to ensure smooth texture. Cover the bowl with plastic wrap, pressing it directly onto the surface of the custard to prevent a skin from forming. Chill in the refrigerator for at least 4 hours or overnight until completely cold.

6. **Churn:**
   - Once chilled, pour the gingerbread custard into an ice cream maker and churn according to the manufacturer's instructions until it reaches a soft-serve consistency.
7. **Add Chopped Gingerbread Cookies:**
   - During the last few minutes of churning, add the chopped gingerbread cookies to the ice cream maker. Let it mix until evenly distributed.
8. **Freeze:**
   - Transfer the churned Gingerbread Ice Cream into an airtight container, pressing a piece of parchment paper directly against the surface of the ice cream to prevent ice crystals from forming. Freeze for at least 4 hours or until firm.
9. **Serve:**
   - Scoop and enjoy your festive Gingerbread Ice Cream! Serve it with additional gingerbread cookie crumbs on top for extra crunch, or enjoy it on its own as a delicious winter dessert that captures the flavors of gingerbread in every creamy bite.

Cherry Cheesecake Ice Cream

Ingredients:

- 2 cups heavy cream
- 1 cup whole milk
- 3/4 cup granulated sugar
- Pinch of salt
- 6 large egg yolks
- 8 ounces cream cheese, softened
- 1 teaspoon vanilla extract
- 1 cup cherry pie filling (homemade or store-bought)
- 1/2 cup graham cracker crumbs

Instructions:

1. **Prepare the Base:**
    - In a medium saucepan, combine the heavy cream, whole milk, half of the sugar (about 6 tablespoons), and salt. Heat over medium heat, stirring occasionally, until it begins to steam and small bubbles form around the edges. Do not let it boil.
2. **Prepare the Cream Cheese Mixture:**
    - In a separate bowl, beat the softened cream cheese until smooth and creamy. Gradually add the remaining sugar (about 6 tablespoons) and beat until well combined.
3. **Temper and Cook the Custard:**
    - In another bowl, whisk the egg yolks until slightly thickened. Gradually whisk in about 1 cup of the warm cream mixture into the egg yolks, a little at a time, to temper the eggs. Pour the tempered egg mixture back into the saucepan with the remaining cream mixture.
    - Cook the custard mixture over medium heat, stirring constantly with a heatproof spatula or wooden spoon, until it thickens slightly and coats the back of the spatula (about 5-7 minutes). Do not let it boil.
4. **Combine Custard with Cream Cheese:**
    - Remove from heat. Gradually whisk the hot custard into the cream cheese mixture until smooth and well combined. Stir in the vanilla extract.
5. **Chill:**
    - Strain the custard through a fine-mesh sieve into a clean bowl to ensure smooth texture. Cover the bowl with plastic wrap, pressing it directly onto

the surface of the custard to prevent a skin from forming. Chill in the refrigerator for at least 4 hours or overnight until completely cold.
6. **Churn:**
    - Once chilled, pour the cheesecake custard into an ice cream maker and churn according to the manufacturer's instructions until it reaches a soft-serve consistency.
7. **Add Cherry Pie Filling and Graham Cracker Crumbs:**
    - During the last few minutes of churning, add the cherry pie filling and graham cracker crumbs to the ice cream maker. Let it mix until evenly distributed.
8. **Freeze:**
    - Transfer the churned Cherry Cheesecake Ice Cream into an airtight container, pressing a piece of parchment paper directly against the surface of the ice cream to prevent ice crystals from forming. Freeze for at least 4 hours or until firm.
9. **Serve:**
    - Scoop and enjoy your delicious Cherry Cheesecake Ice Cream! Serve it with extra graham cracker crumbs on top for added texture, or enjoy it on its own as a delightful dessert that combines the flavors of cheesecake and cherries.

Cookies and Maple Syrup Ice Cream

Ingredients:

- 2 cups heavy cream
- 1 cup whole milk
- 3/4 cup granulated sugar
- 1/2 cup pure maple syrup
- 1 teaspoon vanilla extract
- 1 cup crumbled cookies (e.g., chocolate chip, oatmeal, or maple-flavored)

Instructions:

1. In a mixing bowl, whisk together the heavy cream, whole milk, sugar, maple syrup, and vanilla extract until the sugar is dissolved.
2. Transfer the mixture to an ice cream maker and churn according to the manufacturer's instructions until it reaches a soft-serve consistency.
3. In the last few minutes of churning, add in the crumbled cookies and continue to churn briefly to evenly distribute them.
4. Transfer the ice cream to an airtight container and freeze for at least 4 hours or until firm.
5. Serve scoops of your cookies and maple syrup ice cream in bowls or cones, and enjoy!

This recipe captures the essence of maple syrup and the satisfying crunch of cookies, making it a perfect treat for any ice cream lover.

Carrot Cake Ice Cream

Ingredients:

- 2 cups heavy cream
- 1 cup whole milk
- 3/4 cup granulated sugar
- 1 teaspoon vanilla extract
- 1/2 cup finely grated carrots
- 1/2 cup crushed pineapple, drained
- 1/2 cup chopped walnuts or pecans
- 1/2 cup finely chopped raisins
- 1 teaspoon ground cinnamon
- 1/2 teaspoon ground nutmeg
- 1/4 teaspoon ground cloves
- Cream cheese frosting swirl (optional):
    - 4 oz cream cheese, softened
    - 1/4 cup powdered sugar
    - 1/4 cup heavy cream
- Carrot cake crumbles (optional for additional texture and flavor)

Instructions:

1. In a mixing bowl, whisk together the heavy cream, whole milk, sugar, and vanilla extract until the sugar is dissolved.
2. Stir in the grated carrots, crushed pineapple, chopped nuts, chopped raisins, cinnamon, nutmeg, and cloves until well combined.
3. Transfer the mixture to an ice cream maker and churn according to the manufacturer's instructions until it reaches a soft-serve consistency.
4. If adding a cream cheese frosting swirl, beat the softened cream cheese and powdered sugar together until smooth. Gradually add the heavy cream, beating until smooth and slightly thickened.
5. In the last few minutes of churning the ice cream, drizzle the cream cheese frosting mixture into the ice cream maker to create swirls. Add carrot cake crumbles if desired.
6. Transfer the carrot cake ice cream to an airtight container, layering with additional carrot cake crumbles if desired, and freeze for at least 4 hours or until firm.
7. Serve scoops of carrot cake ice cream in bowls or cones, and enjoy the creamy, spiced flavors reminiscent of carrot cake!

This recipe captures the essence of carrot cake in a frozen treat, perfect for enjoying during warmer months or whenever you're craving a unique twist on a classic dessert.

Fig and Honey Ice Cream

Ingredients:

- 2 cups heavy cream
- 1 cup whole milk
- 3/4 cup honey (preferably mild-flavored like clover honey)
- 1 teaspoon vanilla extract
- Pinch of salt
- 1 cup ripe figs, chopped (about 6-8 figs)
- 1 tablespoon lemon juice

Instructions:

1. In a saucepan, combine the heavy cream, whole milk, honey, vanilla extract, and a pinch of salt. Heat over medium-low heat, stirring occasionally, until the mixture is warm and the honey is completely dissolved. Do not boil.
2. Remove the mixture from heat and let it cool to room temperature.
3. In a separate bowl, mash the chopped figs with lemon juice until they form a coarse puree. You can leave some chunks for texture.
4. Once the cream mixture has cooled, stir in the fig puree until well combined.
5. Transfer the mixture to an ice cream maker and churn according to the manufacturer's instructions until it reaches a soft-serve consistency.
6. Transfer the fig and honey ice cream to an airtight container, smoothing the top. Cover the surface directly with parchment paper or plastic wrap to prevent ice crystals from forming, then seal with the lid.
7. Freeze the ice cream for at least 4 hours or until firm.
8. Serve scoops of fig and honey ice cream in bowls or cones, and enjoy the delicate sweetness and subtle fruity flavor of this unique dessert!

This recipe highlights the natural sweetness of figs complemented by the floral undertones of honey, creating a refreshing and sophisticated ice cream that's perfect for summer or any time you crave a special treat.

Pumpkin Pie Ice Cream

Ingredients:

- 1 cup canned pumpkin puree
- 1 teaspoon ground cinnamon
- 1/2 teaspoon ground ginger
- 1/4 teaspoon ground nutmeg
- 1/4 teaspoon ground cloves
- 2 cups heavy cream
- 1 cup whole milk
- 3/4 cup granulated sugar
- 1 teaspoon vanilla extract
- 1/2 cup graham cracker crumbs (for swirls or to mix in)
- Whipped cream and additional graham cracker crumbs for garnish (optional)

Instructions:

1. In a mixing bowl, whisk together the pumpkin puree, ground cinnamon, ground ginger, ground nutmeg, and ground cloves until well combined. Set aside.
2. In a separate bowl, combine the heavy cream, whole milk, granulated sugar, and vanilla extract. Stir until the sugar is dissolved.
3. Add the pumpkin spice mixture to the cream mixture and whisk until smooth.
4. Transfer the mixture to an ice cream maker and churn according to the manufacturer's instructions until it reaches a soft-serve consistency.
5. If desired, add graham cracker crumbs during the last few minutes of churning to create swirls or mix them into the ice cream for added texture.
6. Transfer the pumpkin pie ice cream to an airtight container, smoothing the top. Cover the surface directly with parchment paper or plastic wrap to prevent ice crystals from forming, then seal with the lid.
7. Freeze the ice cream for at least 4 hours or until firm.
8. Serve scoops of pumpkin pie ice cream in bowls or cones. Optionally, garnish with whipped cream and a sprinkle of graham cracker crumbs for a festive touch.

Enjoy the creamy texture and spiced flavors reminiscent of traditional pumpkin pie in this homemade ice cream treat!

Rice Pudding Ice Cream

Ingredients:

- 1 cup cooked rice (such as Arborio or medium-grain rice)
- 2 cups whole milk
- 1 cup heavy cream
- 1/2 cup granulated sugar
- 1 teaspoon vanilla extract
- 1/2 teaspoon ground cinnamon
- Pinch of salt
- 1/2 cup raisins (optional, soaked in warm water for 10 minutes and drained)
- 1/4 cup chopped nuts (such as almonds or pistachios), toasted (optional)

Instructions:

1. In a saucepan, combine the whole milk, heavy cream, granulated sugar, vanilla extract, ground cinnamon, and a pinch of salt. Heat over medium heat, stirring occasionally, until the mixture starts to simmer. Do not boil.
2. Add the cooked rice to the simmering milk mixture. Stir well to combine.
3. Continue to cook over medium-low heat, stirring frequently, for about 15-20 minutes or until the mixture thickens slightly and coats the back of a spoon.
4. Remove the saucepan from heat and let the rice pudding mixture cool to room temperature.
5. Once cooled, transfer the rice pudding mixture to an airtight container and refrigerate until thoroughly chilled, preferably for at least 2 hours or overnight.
6. Once chilled, transfer the rice pudding mixture to an ice cream maker and churn according to the manufacturer's instructions until it reaches a soft-serve consistency.
7. If desired, stir in soaked and drained raisins and toasted chopped nuts during the last few minutes of churning for added texture and flavor.
8. Transfer the rice pudding ice cream to an airtight container, smoothing the top. Cover the surface directly with parchment paper or plastic wrap to prevent ice crystals from forming, then seal with the lid.
9. Freeze the ice cream for at least 4 hours or until firm.
10. Serve scoops of rice pudding ice cream in bowls or cones, and enjoy the creamy, comforting flavors of this unique dessert!

This recipe captures the essence of rice pudding in a frozen treat, perfect for any occasion where you want to indulge in a comforting and nostalgic dessert.

Rum Raisin Ice Cream

Ingredients:

- 1 cup raisins
- 1/2 cup dark rum
- 2 cups heavy cream
- 1 cup whole milk
- 3/4 cup granulated sugar
- 1 teaspoon vanilla extract
- Pinch of salt

Instructions:

1. In a small bowl, combine the raisins and dark rum. Let them soak for at least 1 hour, stirring occasionally to ensure the raisins absorb the rum.
2. In a saucepan, combine the heavy cream, whole milk, granulated sugar, vanilla extract, and a pinch of salt. Heat over medium heat, stirring occasionally, until the mixture starts to simmer. Do not boil.
3. Remove the saucepan from heat and let the mixture cool to room temperature.
4. Once cooled, strain the rum-soaked raisins, reserving both the raisins and the rum.
5. Stir the reserved rum into the cream mixture until well combined.
6. Transfer the cream mixture to an ice cream maker and churn according to the manufacturer's instructions until it reaches a soft-serve consistency.
7. In the last few minutes of churning, add the strained rum-soaked raisins to the ice cream maker and continue churning briefly to evenly distribute them.
8. Transfer the rum raisin ice cream to an airtight container, smoothing the top. Cover the surface directly with parchment paper or plastic wrap to prevent ice crystals from forming, then seal with the lid.
9. Freeze the ice cream for at least 4 hours or until firm.
10. Serve scoops of rum raisin ice cream in bowls or cones, and enjoy the creamy texture and rich flavors of this classic dessert!

This recipe captures the essence of rum raisin ice cream, with the rum-infused raisins adding a delightful boozy flavor that complements the creamy base perfectly.

Bourbon Pecan Ice Cream

Ingredients:

- 1 cup pecans, chopped
- 2 tablespoons unsalted butter
- 1/4 cup bourbon
- 2 cups heavy cream
- 1 cup whole milk
- 3/4 cup granulated sugar
- Pinch of salt
- 1 teaspoon vanilla extract

Instructions:

1. In a skillet, melt the unsalted butter over medium heat. Add the chopped pecans and toast them, stirring frequently, until they are fragrant and lightly browned. This should take about 5-7 minutes. Be careful not to burn them. Remove from heat and set aside to cool.
2. In a saucepan, combine the heavy cream, whole milk, granulated sugar, and a pinch of salt. Heat over medium heat, stirring occasionally, until the mixture starts to simmer. Do not boil.
3. Remove the saucepan from heat and let the mixture cool to room temperature.
4. Once cooled, stir in the bourbon and vanilla extract until well combined.
5. Transfer the cream mixture to an ice cream maker and churn according to the manufacturer's instructions until it reaches a soft-serve consistency.
6. In the last few minutes of churning, add the toasted pecans to the ice cream maker and continue churning briefly to evenly distribute them.
7. Transfer the bourbon pecan ice cream to an airtight container, smoothing the top. Cover the surface directly with parchment paper or plastic wrap to prevent ice crystals from forming, then seal with the lid.
8. Freeze the ice cream for at least 4 hours or until firm.
9. Serve scoops of bourbon pecan ice cream in bowls or cones, and enjoy the creamy texture and rich, boozy flavors of this indulgent dessert!

This recipe captures the essence of bourbon pecan ice cream, with the toasted pecans adding a delightful crunch and the bourbon lending a warm, caramel-like flavor to the creamy base.

Cardamom Pistachio Ice Cream

Ingredients:

- 1 cup shelled pistachios, unsalted
- 2 cups heavy cream
- 1 cup whole milk
- 3/4 cup granulated sugar
- 1 teaspoon ground cardamom
- Pinch of salt
- 1 teaspoon vanilla extract

Instructions:

1. Toast the pistachios: Preheat your oven to 350°F (175°C). Spread the pistachios on a baking sheet in a single layer. Toast them in the oven for about 8-10 minutes, until lightly golden and fragrant. Stir occasionally to ensure even toasting. Remove from the oven and let them cool completely. Once cooled, roughly chop them and set aside.
2. In a saucepan, combine the heavy cream, whole milk, granulated sugar, ground cardamom, and a pinch of salt. Heat over medium heat, stirring occasionally, until the mixture just begins to simmer. Do not boil.
3. Remove the saucepan from heat and let the mixture cool to room temperature.
4. Once cooled, stir in the vanilla extract and chopped toasted pistachios until well combined.
5. Transfer the cream mixture to an ice cream maker and churn according to the manufacturer's instructions until it reaches a soft-serve consistency.
6. Transfer the cardamom pistachio ice cream to an airtight container, smoothing the top. Cover the surface directly with parchment paper or plastic wrap to prevent ice crystals from forming, then seal with the lid.
7. Freeze the ice cream for at least 4 hours or until firm.
8. Serve scoops of cardamom pistachio ice cream in bowls or cones, and enjoy the creamy texture and aromatic flavors of this unique dessert!

This recipe captures the aromatic essence of cardamom and the crunchy texture of pistachios, making it a refreshing and flavorful treat for any occasion.

Earl Grey Tea Ice Cream

Ingredients:

- 2 cups heavy cream
- 1 cup whole milk
- 3/4 cup granulated sugar
- 3-4 Earl Grey tea bags (or loose tea equivalent)
- Pinch of salt
- 5 large egg yolks
- 1 teaspoon vanilla extract

Instructions:

1. In a saucepan, combine the heavy cream, whole milk, granulated sugar, Earl Grey tea bags (or loose tea in a tea infuser), and a pinch of salt. Heat over medium heat, stirring occasionally, until the mixture just begins to simmer. Remove from heat and let it steep for 15-20 minutes to infuse the tea flavor. Taste occasionally to ensure the desired strength of tea flavor.
2. In a separate bowl, whisk the egg yolks until smooth.
3. Gradually pour the warm cream mixture into the egg yolks, whisking constantly, to temper the eggs. This step prevents the eggs from cooking too quickly.
4. Pour the egg and cream mixture back into the saucepan. Cook over medium heat, stirring constantly with a wooden spoon or spatula, until the mixture thickens slightly and coats the back of the spoon. This usually takes about 5-7 minutes, and the mixture should reach a temperature of around 170°F (77°C) for proper thickening.
5. Remove the saucepan from heat and strain the mixture through a fine-mesh sieve into a clean bowl to remove the tea leaves and any bits of cooked egg.
6. Stir in the vanilla extract. Let the mixture cool to room temperature, then cover with plastic wrap, pressing it directly onto the surface of the custard to prevent a skin from forming.
7. Refrigerate the custard until completely chilled, preferably overnight.
8. Once chilled, churn the custard in an ice cream maker according to the manufacturer's instructions until it reaches a soft-serve consistency.
9. Transfer the Earl Grey tea ice cream to an airtight container, smoothing the top. Cover the surface directly with parchment paper or plastic wrap to prevent ice crystals from forming, then seal with the lid.
10. Freeze the ice cream for at least 4 hours or until firm.

11. Serve scoops of Earl Grey tea ice cream in bowls or cones, and enjoy the delicate floral and citrusy flavors of this unique dessert!

This recipe captures the essence of Earl Grey tea in a creamy and refreshing ice cream, perfect for tea lovers and dessert enthusiasts alike.

Chai Spice Ice Cream

Ingredients:

- 2 cups heavy cream
- 1 cup whole milk
- 1/2 cup granulated sugar
- 4-5 chai tea bags (or loose chai tea equivalent)
- 1 teaspoon vanilla extract
- 1/2 teaspoon ground cinnamon
- 1/4 teaspoon ground ginger
- 1/4 teaspoon ground cardamom
- 1/8 teaspoon ground cloves
- Pinch of ground black pepper (optional)
- Pinch of salt
- 5 large egg yolks

Instructions:

1. In a saucepan, combine the heavy cream, whole milk, granulated sugar, chai tea bags (or loose tea in a tea infuser), vanilla extract, ground cinnamon, ground ginger, ground cardamom, ground cloves, ground black pepper (if using), and a pinch of salt. Heat over medium heat, stirring occasionally, until the mixture just begins to simmer. Remove from heat and let it steep for 15-20 minutes to infuse the chai tea and spices. Taste occasionally to ensure the desired strength of chai flavor.
2. In a separate bowl, whisk the egg yolks until smooth.
3. Gradually pour the warm chai-infused cream mixture into the egg yolks, whisking constantly, to temper the eggs. This step prevents the eggs from cooking too quickly.
4. Pour the egg and cream mixture back into the saucepan. Cook over medium heat, stirring constantly with a wooden spoon or spatula, until the mixture thickens slightly and coats the back of the spoon. This usually takes about 5-7 minutes, and the mixture should reach a temperature of around 170°F (77°C) for proper thickening.
5. Remove the saucepan from heat and strain the mixture through a fine-mesh sieve into a clean bowl to remove the tea leaves and any bits of cooked egg.
6. Let the mixture cool to room temperature, then cover with plastic wrap, pressing it directly onto the surface of the custard to prevent a skin from forming.
7. Refrigerate the chai spice custard until completely chilled, preferably overnight.

8. Once chilled, churn the custard in an ice cream maker according to the manufacturer's instructions until it reaches a soft-serve consistency.
9. Transfer the chai spice ice cream to an airtight container, smoothing the top. Cover the surface directly with parchment paper or plastic wrap to prevent ice crystals from forming, then seal with the lid.
10. Freeze the ice cream for at least 4 hours or until firm.
11. Serve scoops of chai spice ice cream in bowls or cones, and enjoy the warm, aromatic flavors reminiscent of a comforting cup of chai tea!

This recipe captures the complex and comforting flavors of chai tea in a creamy ice cream, making it a delightful dessert for chai lovers and those looking to try something new and flavorful.

Chocolate Chip Cookie Dough Ice Cream

Ingredients:

For the cookie dough:

- 1/2 cup unsalted butter, softened
- 1/4 cup granulated sugar
- 1/2 cup packed light brown sugar
- 2 tablespoons milk
- 1/2 teaspoon vanilla extract
- 1 cup all-purpose flour
- 1/4 teaspoon salt
- 1/2 cup mini chocolate chips

For the ice cream base:

- 2 cups heavy cream
- 1 cup whole milk
- 3/4 cup granulated sugar
- 1 teaspoon vanilla extract
- Pinch of salt

Instructions:

To make the cookie dough:

1. In a mixing bowl, beat the softened butter, granulated sugar, and brown sugar together until creamy and smooth.
2. Mix in the milk and vanilla extract until well combined.
3. Gradually add the flour and salt, mixing until fully incorporated and a dough forms.
4. Fold in the mini chocolate chips until evenly distributed throughout the cookie dough.
5. Shape the cookie dough into small, bite-sized balls (about 1/2-inch in diameter). Place them on a parchment-lined baking sheet and freeze until firm, at least 1 hour.

To make the ice cream:

1. In a saucepan, combine the heavy cream, whole milk, granulated sugar, vanilla extract, and a pinch of salt. Heat over medium heat, stirring occasionally, until the mixture just begins to simmer. Remove from heat.
2. Let the mixture cool to room temperature.
3. Once cooled, transfer the ice cream base to an ice cream maker and churn according to the manufacturer's instructions until it reaches a soft-serve consistency.
4. In the last few minutes of churning, add the frozen cookie dough balls to the ice cream maker and continue churning briefly to evenly distribute them.
5. Transfer the chocolate chip cookie dough ice cream to an airtight container, smoothing the top. Cover the surface directly with parchment paper or plastic wrap to prevent ice crystals from forming, then seal with the lid.
6. Freeze the ice cream for at least 4 hours or until firm.
7. Serve scoops of chocolate chip cookie dough ice cream in bowls or cones, and enjoy the creamy vanilla base studded with chunks of cookie dough and chocolate chips!

This recipe captures the indulgent flavors and textures of chocolate chip cookie dough ice cream, making it a perfect homemade treat for ice cream enthusiasts of all ages.

Neapolitan Ice Cream

Ingredients:

Vanilla Layer:

- 1 cup heavy cream
- 1 cup whole milk
- 1/2 cup granulated sugar
- 1 teaspoon vanilla extract

Chocolate Layer:

- 1 cup heavy cream
- 1 cup whole milk
- 1/2 cup granulated sugar
- 1/4 cup unsweetened cocoa powder
- 1/2 teaspoon vanilla extract

Strawberry Layer:

- 1 cup heavy cream
- 1 cup whole milk
- 1/2 cup granulated sugar
- 1/2 cup strawberry puree (fresh or frozen strawberries blended until smooth)
- 1/2 teaspoon vanilla extract

Instructions:

For each layer (Vanilla, Chocolate, and Strawberry):

1. In a saucepan, combine the heavy cream, whole milk, and granulated sugar. Heat over medium heat, stirring occasionally, until the mixture just begins to simmer. Do not boil.
2. Remove from heat and stir in the respective flavorings:
    - For the **Vanilla Layer**: Stir in 1 teaspoon vanilla extract. Let cool to room temperature.
    - For the **Chocolate Layer**: Stir in the cocoa powder and 1/2 teaspoon vanilla extract until the cocoa powder is fully dissolved. Let cool to room temperature.
    - For the **Strawberry Layer**: Stir in the strawberry puree and 1/2 teaspoon vanilla extract until well combined. Let cool to room temperature.

3. Once each layer mixture has cooled, transfer them to separate containers and refrigerate until thoroughly chilled, preferably for at least 2 hours or overnight.

Assembly:

1. Once chilled, pour each mixture into the compartments of an ice cream maker and churn according to the manufacturer's instructions until each layer reaches a soft-serve consistency. If you don't have compartments, churn each flavor separately.
2. Assemble the Neapolitan ice cream in layers in an airtight container, alternating between vanilla, chocolate, and strawberry. You can use a loaf pan or similar container to create distinct layers.
3. After assembling the layers, cover the ice cream with parchment paper or plastic wrap directly on the surface to prevent ice crystals from forming. Seal with the lid.
4. Freeze the Neapolitan ice cream for at least 4 hours or until firm.
5. To serve, scoop the Neapolitan ice cream into bowls or cones, and enjoy the classic combination of vanilla, chocolate, and strawberry flavors!

This homemade Neapolitan ice cream recipe allows you to enjoy the nostalgic flavors of this classic dessert with the satisfaction of making it from scratch.

www.ingramcontent.com/pod-product-compliance
Lightning Source LLC
LaVergne TN
LVHW061942070526
838199LV00060B/3935